D0330567

1001
EASY
SPANISH
PHRASES

Pablo García Loaeza, Ph.D.

DOVER PUBLICATIONS, Garden City, New York

Bibliographical Note

1001 Easy Spanish Phrases is a new work, first published by
Dover Publications in 2010.

Library of Congress Cataloging-in-Publication Data

Loaeza, Pablo García, 1972–
  1001 easy Spanish phrases / Pablo García Loaeza.
    p. cm. (Dover language guides)
  ISBN-13: 978-0-486-47619-3
  ISBN-10: 0-486-47619-7
    1. Spanish language—Conversation and phrase books—English.
I. Title. II. Title: One thousand one easy Spanish phrases. III. Title:
One thousand and one easy Spanish phrases.
PC4121.P33 2010
468.3'421—dc22

                                                          2010018979

Manufactured in the United States of America
ScoutAutomatedPrintCode
www.doverpublications.com

Contents

iv Contents

Introduction

This book will let you become familiar with a basic set of sentences, phrases, and words for simple everyday communication in Spanish. In particular, the would-be visitor to a Spanish-speaking country will find the tools necessary to deal with common situations related to travel abroad. The different sections cover topics such as transportation, accommodation, eating and drinking, as well as sightseeing, and shopping. There are also sections that cover a number of problems that may arise. Each section takes account of dialectic variation in Spanish by pointing out when a specific word is used in Spain (Sp.) or a particular Latin American country (Mex., Arg., etc.). When appropriate, entries indicate whether the corresponding Spanish sentence is formal (for.) or informal (inf.).

The book was designed to serve as a useful foundation rather than an exhaustive field manual. It is meant to be used for reference, study, and review. The more you practice the essential structures included here, the easier it will be for you to generate the questions and statements appropriate to your specific needs and circumstances. When you are communicating with someone, the other person is also trying to make sense of what you are saying and drawing information not just from your words, but also from context, tone of voice, and body language. When you need an answer, looking a person in the eye is generally more practical and more effective than reading from a book.

To facilitate acquisition, the material included in the different sections is presented in a logical sequence. As you go through the sentences, imagine yourself in the situations they suggest. In the "Eating & Drinking" section, for instance, you can go from finding a restaurant to asking for the check after ordering breakfast, lunch or dinner, and dessert. Since the material is not cumulative, book sections can be studied according to need or preference. You will note that certain structures, such as "I want . . ." and "where is . . . ," appear frequently throughout the book. Besides being very handy, their repetition facilitates focusing on the many complementary words and phrases. Thus, you can learn to produce a large number of sentences and convey a wide range of information with minimum effort.

Finally, while practice trumps theory, the Spanish Grammar Primer included here will help you make the most of the book. Besides vocabulary-building tips and verb conjugation tables, it contains information about nouns, adjectives, pronouns, and prepositions. However, many people will find Dover's *Essential Spanish Grammar* (ISBN 0-486-20780-3) helpful for mastering the subtleties of the Spanish language. Likewise, *2,001 Most Useful Spanish Words* (ISBN 0-486-47616-2), also published by Dover, is a useful complement for increasing your Spanish vocabulary further.

A Note on Spanish Dialects

As with English, there are many regional dialects of Spanish. They may vary in pronunciation, vocabulary, and syntax but they are all mutually intelligible.

For instance, in the Castile region of Spain a "c" before an "e" or an "i" sounds like "th" in English and the letter "s" is pronounced like "sh." On the other hand, people in the south of Spain and in Latin America, generally make the letter "c" (before "e" or "i"), the letter "s," and even the letter "z" all sound like the "s" in "soup." Caribbean Spanish tends to drop a "d" between two vowels at the end of some words, as well as a final "s" so that *cansados* (tired, m. pl.) becomes *cansao*. Likewise, in many South American countries the word for cake is *torta*, whereas in Mexico it is *pastel*. In Latin America a computer is called *una computadora* while in Spain it is referred to as *un ordenador*. Nevertheless, a Spaniard, a Mexican, a Chilean, and a Dominican can engage in conversation without impediment.

When Spanish is learned as a second language the choice of dialect can depend on personal interest and circumstance. For example, someone traveling to Spain might prefer to become familiar with the Castilian dialect, while someone spending time in a Latin American country will pick up the local accent and lingo. The best investment for a beginner studying stateside is to practice a "neutral" kind of Spanish: all the syllables in a word should be pronounced clearly, using the standard word-stress rules (see the grammar section). Once you know the basic system, a little practice makes it easy to compensate for dialectical differences. Remember also that the most useful words, such as *por favor* and *gracias*, are the same throughout the Spanish-speaking world.

Unlike English—in which the same word may be written one way in Britain (colour, dialogue, emphasise, gaol) and another in the United States (color, dialog, emphasize, jail), all Spanish dialects use the same written standard.

Phonetic Transcription

The phonetic transcription of the Spanish words and phrases is provided as an aid to an approximately correct pronunciation in the absence of an audio model. However, the Spanish sound scheme is very regular and straightforward; with some practice you should be able to bypass the phonetic transcription in most instances.

Other than the International Phonetic Alphabet, which employs a special set of characters, there is no standard for phonetic transcription. In order to facilitate reading, the phonetic transcription in this book follows the rules of English pronunciation and spelling as closely as possible. For instance, vowels are short before a double consonant (as in "dress"); the letter "c" is hard before an "a" or an "o" (as in "car"), but soft before an "e" (as in "celery"); etc. The syllables that should be stressed are underlined.

The phonetic transcription presented here corresponds to a "neutral" dialect of Spanish which, pronounced correctly, will be understood in any Spanish-speaking country.

Phonetic transcription key:

ah	A as in father and drama.
ay	long A as in stay, weigh, and train.
ch	as in chat, chess, and cheese.
ee	long E as in feet and eel.
eh, ess	short E as in pet, let, less, and rest.
ehr	sounds like air.
g	hard G as in gap, get, and geese.*
h	H as in ham, heel, and hot.
I, i	long I as in the first person pronoun.
k	hard C as in cat, cot, and cool, or K as in king.

* In Spanish an intervocalic G tends towards vocalization and will be represented by a "w" in order to reflect actual pronunciation better. For example, *agua* (water) will be transcripted as "<u>ah</u>-wah."

ny	as in bar**ny**ard and ca**ny**on.
oh	long O as in h**o**pe, **o**pen, and c**o**ne.
oo	OO as in m**oo**n and s**oo**n.
oy	as in b**oy**, s**oy**, and t**oy**.
s	as in **s**at, **s**et, or soft C as in **c**ellar and **c**entral.
w	as in **w**ell and **w**et.
y	as in **y**ard and **y**et.

Spanish Pronunciation

Vowels

Spanish only has five vowel sounds (English has over 15!) which correspond to the five vowel letters, regardless of their position in a word. There are no silent vowels in Spanish. The five vowel sounds in Spanish are:

a as in dr**a**ma	*Habla a la casa blanca.*	Call the White House.
e as in b**e**t	*Él es el rebelde René Pérez.*	He is the rebel René Pérez.
i as in d**ee**p	*Sí, viví sin ti.*	Yes, I lived without you.
o as in c**oa**t	*Los locos no son tontos.*	Crazy people aren't dumb.
u as in l**oo**p	*Fui a un club nocturno.*	I went to a nightclub.

The semi-consonant y is pronounced like i [ee] when used as a conjunction: Pedro y María (*Pedro and María*); its sound softens next to a vowel (as in yellow): Juan y yo somos muy buenos amigos (*Juan and I are very good friends*).

Consonants

Spanish has basically the same consonant sounds as English. However, there are a few particulars to keep in mind:

b and v are very often pronounced the same way, as in "bee."

c (soft), s, and z vary in pronunciation in some Spanish dialects. However, in all but the rarest cases, they can all be pronounced like the s in "soft" without risk of confusion.

g is hard as in good before a, o, and u, but soft as in horse before e or i.

gu is used before e and i to represent a hard g sound as in good (note

that here the **u** does not function as a vowel; **gu** is a digraph in
which two letters represent a single sound as in th**e**).

h is always mute as in **h**erbs.

j is pronounced like the **h** in **h**orse.

ll is always pronounced as the **y** in **y**ellow.

ñ represents a particular sound which resembles the **ny** combination
found in ca**ny**on.

qu is used before **e** and **i** to represent a hard **c** sound as in **c**at (see **gu**
above).

r at the beginning of a word is trilled.

rr represents a trill in the middle of a word.

Stress and written accents

Spanish words tend to have two or more syllables; when they are pronounced one syllable always sounds a little bit louder than the others.
The stressed syllable is either the last, the penultimate (most often),
or the antepenultimate syllable (least often). Word stress in Spanish is
determined by two simple rules:

1. Words that end in a **vowel**, **n**, or **s** are generally pronounced
   stressing the **next to last syllable**:
   Ven**ta**na (*window*), **bar**co (*boat*), pa**lab**ras (*words*), tú **can**tas
   (*you sing*), ellos **com**en (*they eat*)
2. Words which end in a **consonant** other than **n** or **s** are generally
   stressed on the **last syllable**:
   pa**pel** (*paper*), fe**liz** (*happy*), acti**tud** (*attitude*), can**tar** (*to sing*),
   com**er** (*to eat*)

Written accent marks are used when a word's pronunciation is at
odds with these rules. In other words, accent marks indicate a stress
where you wouldn't normally expect it.

Thus, words which end in a vowel, **n**, or **s** but require the stress to
fall on the last syllable need a written accent mark to "drag" the sound
forward:

ciem**piés** (*centipede*), can**ción** (*song*), él can**tó** (*he sang*),* yo co**mí**
(*I ate*)

_____

* Note the difference with yo **canto** (*I sing*): a change in stress can significantly change
the meaning of a word or even a whole sentence.

Conversely, words that need the stress to fall on the next to last syllable but end in a consonant other than **n** or **s** need a written accent mark to "drag" the sound backward:

lápiz (*pencil*), árbol (*tree*), azúcar (*sugar*), carácter (*character*)

Finally, words that need the stress on the antepenultimate syllable always have a written accent:

murciélago (*bat*)*, círculo (*circle*), lágrima (*eye tear*), cántalo (*sing it*)

---

* Repeating the word **murciélago** out loud is a good way to practice pronunciation: it has all five vowel sounds and distinctive stress.

1001
EASY
SPANISH
PHRASES

NUMBERS

zero	*cero*	<u>seh</u>-roh
one	*uno*	<u>oo</u>-noh
two	*dos*	dohss
three	*tres*	trehss
four	*cuatro*	<u>kwah</u>-troh
five	*cinco*	<u>seen</u>-koh
six	*seis*	<u>sayss</u>
seven	*siete*	see-<u>eh</u>-teh
eight	*ocho*	<u>oh</u>-choh
nine	*nueve*	<u>nweh</u>-veh
ten	*diez*	dee-<u>ess</u>
eleven	*once*	<u>ohn</u>-seh
twelve	*doce*	<u>doh</u>-seh
thirteen	*trece*	<u>treh</u>-seh
fourteen	*catorce*	kah-<u>tor</u>-seh
fifteen	*quince*	<u>keen</u>-seh
sixteen	*dieciséis*	dee-eh-see-<u>sayss</u>
seventeen	*diecisiete*	dee-eh-see-see-<u>eh</u>-teh
eighteen	*dieciocho*	dee-eh-see-<u>oh</u>-choh
nineteen	*diecinueve*	dee-eh-see-<u>nweh</u>-veh
twenty	*veinte*	<u>vayn</u>-teh
twenty-one	*veintiuno*	vayn-tee-<u>oo</u>-noh
twenty-two	*veintidós*	vayn-tee-<u>dohss</u>
thirty	*treinta*	<u>trayn</u>-tah
thirty-one	*treinta y uno*	<u>trayn</u>-tah ee <u>oo</u>-noh
thirty-two	*treinta y dos*	<u>trayn</u>-tah ee dohss

forty	*cuarenta*	kwah-<u>ren</u>-tah
fifty	*cincuenta*	seen-<u>kwen</u>-tah
sixty	*sesenta*	seh-<u>sen</u>-tah
seventy	*setenta*	seh-<u>ten</u>-tah
eighty	*ochenta*	oh-<u>chen</u>-tah
ninety	*noventa*	noh-<u>ven</u>-tah
one hundred	*cien*	see-<u>en</u>
one hundred and one	*ciento uno*	see-<u>en</u>-toh <u>oo</u>-noh
one hundred and two	*ciento dos*	see-<u>en</u>-toh dohss
two hundred	*doscientos*	dohss-see-<u>en</u>-tohss
three hundred	*trescientos*	trehss-see-<u>en</u>-tohss
four hundred	*cuatrocientos*	kwah-troh-see-<u>en</u>-tohss
five hundred	*quinientos*	kee-nee-<u>en</u>-tohss
six hundred	*seiscientos*	sayss-see-<u>en</u>-tohss
seven hundred	*setecientos*	seh-teh-see-<u>en</u>-tohss
eight hundred	*ochocientos*	oh-choh-see-<u>en</u>-tohss
nine hundred	*novecientos*	noh-veh-see-<u>en</u>-tohss
one thousand	*mil*	meel
two thousand	*dos mil*	dohss-<u>meel</u>
one hundred thousand	*cien mil*	see-<u>en</u> meel
million	*millón*	mee-<u>yohn</u>
two million	*dos millones*	dohss mee-<u>yoh</u>-ness

1. I need to add up these numbers.
   Necesito sumar estos números.
   Neh-seh-<u>see</u>-toh soo-<u>mar</u> ess-tohss <u>noo</u>-meh-rohss

2. How much is one plus one?   *¿Cuánto es uno más uno?*
   <u>Kwahn</u>-toh ess <u>oo</u>-noh mahss <u>oo</u>-noh

3. What's the total?   *¿Cuál es el total?*   Kwahl ess el toh-<u>tahl</u>

4. What happens if I multiply it by two?
   ¿Qué pasa si lo multiplico por dos?
   Keh <u>pah</u>-sah see loh mool-tee-<u>plee</u>-koh por dohss

5. Can I divide it by three?   *¿Lo puedo dividir por tres?*
   Loh <u>pweh</u>-doh dee-vee-<u>deer</u> por trehss

6. Now take away one.   *Ahora réstale uno.*
   Ah-<u>oh</u>-rah <u>ress</u>-tah-leh <u>oo</u>-noh

7. These numbers don't add up!   *¡Estos números están mal!*
   <u>Ess</u>-tohss <u>noo</u>-meh-rohss ess-<u>tahn</u> mahl

COLORS

8. What's your favorite color?   *¿Cuál es tu color favorito?*
   Kwahl ess too koh-<u>lor</u> fah-voh-<u>ree</u>-toh

9. My favorite color is blue.   *Mi color favorito es azul.*
   Mee koh-<u>lor</u> fah-voh-<u>ree</u>-toh ess ah-<u>sool</u>

. . . black.	. . . *negro.*	neh-groh
. . . brown.	. . . *café/marrón.*	kah-<u>feh</u>/mah-<u>ron</u>
. . . green.	. . . *verde.*	<u>vehr</u>-deh
. . . gray.	. . . *gris.*	greess
. . . orange.	. . . *anaranjado.*	ah-nah-rahn-<u>hah</u>-doh
. . . pink.	. . . *rosa.*	<u>roh</u>-sah
. . . purple.	. . . *morado.*	moh-<u>rah</u>-doh
. . . red.	. . . *rojo.*	<u>roh</u>-hoh
. . . white.	. . . *blanco.*	<u>blahn</u>-koh
. . . yellow.	. . . *amarillo.*	ah-mah-<u>ree</u>-yoh

10. What color is . . .   *¿De qué color es . . . ?*
    Deh keh koh-<u>lor</u> ess

MEETING & GREETING

11. Hello.   *Hola.*   <u>Oh</u>-lah

12. Good morning/day.   *Buenos días.*   <u>Bweh</u>-nohss <u>dee</u>-ahss

13. Good afternoon.   *Buenas tardes.*   **Bweh**-nahss **tar**-dess

14. Good evening/night.   *Buenas noches.*
     Bweh-nahss **noh**-chess

15. Welcome.   *Bienvenido/-a(s).*   **Bee-en-veh-nee**-doh/-ah(ss)

16. Come in.   *Adelante./Pase(n).*   **Ah-dehl-ahn**-teh/**Pah**-seh(n)

17. Don't be shy.   *No tenga(n) pena.*   **Noh ten**-gah(n) **peh**-nah

18. Pleased to meet you.   *Es un placer (conocerlo/-a).*
     Ess oon plah-sehr (koh-noh-**sehr**-loh/-ah)

19. Nice to meet you.   *Mucho gusto (en conocerlo/-a).*
     Moo-choh **goos**-toh (en koh-noh-**sehr**-loh/-ah)

20. The pleasure is mine.   *El gusto es mío.*
     El goos-toh ess **mee**-oh

21. Charmed.   *Encantado.*   **En-kahn-tah**-doh

22. Likewise.   *Igualmente.*   **Ee-wahl-men**-teh

23. What's your name? (for.)   *¿Cómo se llama (usted)?*
     Koh-moh seh **yah**-mah (oos-**ted**)

24. What's your name? (inf.)   *. . . te llamas?*   teh **yah**-mahss

25. I'm called . . .   *Me llamo . . .*   Meh **yah**-moh

26. My name is . . .   *Mi nombre es . . .*
     Mee **nohm**-breh ess . . .

27. Where are you from? (for./inf.)   *¿De dónde es/eres?*
     Deh **dohn**-deh ess/ **eh**-ress

28. I'm from . . .   *Soy de . . .*   Soy deh

29. Let me introduce you to . . . (for./inf.)
     Le/te presento a . . .   Leh/teh preh-**sen**-toh ah

30. How are you? (for./inf.)   *¿Cómo está(s)?*
     Koh-moh ess-**tahss**

31. How's it going? (for./inf.)   *¿Cómo le/te va?*
     Koh-moh leh/teh vah

32. How goes it?   *¿Qué tal?*   **Keh tahl**

33. Very well/Fine, thank you.   *(Muy) Bien, gracias.*
    (Mooy) Bee-en, grah-see-ahss

34. So-so.   *Más o menos./Así así. (Sp.)*
    Mahss oh meh-nohss/Ah-see ah-see

35. (Very) bad.   *(Muy) Mal.*   **(Mooy) Mahl**

36. And yourself? (for./inf.)   *¿Y usted/tú?*   **Ee oos-ted/too**

37. What's new?   *¿Qué hay de nuevo?*   **Keh I deh nweh-voh**

38. What's going on?   *¿Qué pasó?/¿Qué hubo? (L. Am.)*
    Keh pah-soh/Keh oo-boh

39. What's happening?   *¿Qué pasa?/¿Qué onda? (Mex.)*
    Keh pah-sah/Keh ohn-dah

40. All's well.   *Todo bien./Todo cheque. (Hon.)*
    Toh-doh bee-en/Toh-doh cheh-keh

41. I don't know.   *No sé.*   **Noh seh**

42. Nothing.   *Nada.*   **Nah-dah**

43. Good-bye.   *Adiós.*   **Ah-dee-ohss**

44. I don't like good-byes.   *No me gustan las despedidas.*
    No meh goos-tahn lahss dess-peh-dee-dahss

45. See you later.   *Nos vemos./Hasta luego.*
    Nohss veh-mohss/Ahss-tah lweh-goh

46. See you soon.   *Hasta pronto.*   **Ahss-tah prohn-toh**

47. See you tomorrow.   *Hasta mañana.*
    Ahss-tah mah-nyah-nah

48. Until we meet again.   *Hasta la vista/la próxima.*
    Ahss-tah lah vees-tah/lah prohk-see-mah

49. When will we meet again?   *¿Cuándo nos volveremos a ver?*
    Kwahn-doh nohss vohl-veh-reh-mohss ah vehr

50. Hopefully it won't be long.   *Ojalá no pase mucho tiempo.*
    Oh-hah-**lah** noh **pah**-seh **moo**-choh tee-**em**-poh

51. Have a nice day.   *Que te vaya bien.*
    Keh teh **vah**-yah bee-**en**

52. I hope you had a good time.   *Espero que se hayan divertido.*
    Ess-**peh**-roh keh seh **I**-ahn dee-vehr-**tee**-doh

53. I had a lot of fun.   *Me divertí mucho.*
    Meh dee-vehr-**tee** **moo**-choh

54. I had a (very) good time.   *La pasé (muy) bien.*
    Lah pah-**seh** (mooy) bee-**en**

55. Come back soon!   *¡Regresen pronto!*
    Reh-**greh**-sen-**prohn**-toh

56. Don't come back!   *¡No vuelvan!*   Noh **vwel**-vahn

57. Good luck.   *(Buena) Suerte.*   (**Bweh**-nah) **Swehr**-teh

58. Take care.   *Cuídate.*   Kwee-**dah**-teh

59. Give my regards to . . .   *Saludos a . . .*   Sah-**loo**-dohss ah

BASIC COURTESY

60. Please.   *Por favor.*   Por fah-**vor**

61. Thank you (very much).   *(Muchas) Gracias.*
    (**Moo**-chahss) **Grah**-see-ahss

62. Thanks for everything.   *Gracias por todo.*
    Grah-see-ahss por **toh**-doh

63. I'm very grateful. (for.)   *Se lo agradezco mucho.*
    Seh loh ah-grah-**dess**-koh **moo**-choh

64. You're welcome.   *De nada./No hay de qué.*
    Deh **nah**-dah/Noh I deh keh

65. Excuse me. (for.)   *Disculpe./Perdóneme.*
    Dees-**kool**-peh/Pehr-**doh**-neh-meh

66. If I may be allowed. *Con permiso.* **Kohn pehr-mee-soh**

67. I wouldn't want to bother you. (for.)
No quisiera molestarlo. **Noh kee-see-eh-rah moh-less-tar-loh**

68. I didn't mean to . . . *No era mi intención . . .*
Noh eh-rah mee een-ten-see-ohn

69. I hope it's not too much of a bother.
Espero que no sea mucha molestia
Ess-peh-roh keh noh seh-ah moo-chah moh-less-tee-ah

70. If you don't mind. *Si no le importa.*
See noh leh eem-por-tah

71. I would like to . . . *Me gustaría . . .* **Meh goos-tah-ree-ah**

72. May I . . . ? *¿Puedo . . . ?* **Pweh-doh**

73. Is one allowed to . . . ? *¿Se puede . . . ?* **Seh pweh-deh**

74. Sure, absolutely. *¿Cómo no?* **Koh-moh noh**

75. It's ok. *Está bien.* **Ess-tah bee-en**

76. No problem. *No hay problema.* **Noh I proh-bleh-mah**

77. Of course. *No faltaba más.* **Noh fahl-tah-bah mahss**

78. Allow me. (for.) *Permítame.* **Pehr-mee-tah-meh**

79. Gladly. *Con gusto.* **Kohn goos-toh**

80. Don't bother. (for.) *No se moleste.* **Noh seh moh-less-teh**

81. Don't worry. (for.) *No se preocupe.*
Noh seh preh-oh-koo-peh

82. I'm sorry. *Lo siento.* **Loh see-en-toh**

83. Bless you. *Salud.* **Sah-lood**

HOW DO YOU SAY . . . ?

84. Do you speak English? (for./inf.)
    ¿Habla(s) inglés?   <u>Ah</u>-blah(s) een-<u>gless</u>

85. Does anyone here speak English?
    ¿Alguien aquí habla inglés?
    Ahl-gee-<u>en</u> ah-<u>kee</u> <u>ah</u>-blah een-<u>gless</u>

86. Do you understand me? (for./inf.)   *¿Me entiende(s)?*
    Meh en-tee-<u>en</u>-deh(ss)

87. I don't understand.   *No entiendo/comprendo.*
    Noh en-tee-<u>en</u>-doh/kohm-<u>pren</u>-doh

88. I'm confused.   *Estoy confundido.*
    Ess-<u>toy</u> kohn-foon-<u>dee</u>-doh

89. I don't speak Spanish.   *No hablo español.*
    Noh <u>ah</u>-bloh ess-pah-<u>nyohl</u>

90. I speak a little Spanish.   *Hablo un poco de español.*
    <u>Ah</u>-bloh oon <u>poh</u>-koh deh ess-pah-<u>nyohl</u>

91. I don't know this word.   *No conozco esta palabra.*
    Noh koh-<u>nohss</u>-koh <u>ess</u>-tah pah-<u>lah</u>-brah

92. I didn't hear you correctly. (for.)   *No lo escuché bien.*
    Noh loh ess-koo-<u>cheh</u> bee-<u>en</u>

93. Say again, please. (for.)   *Repita, por favor.*
    Reh-<u>pee</u>-tah, por fah-<u>vor</u>

94. Not so fast.   *No tan rápido.*   Noh tahn <u>rah</u>-pee-doh.

95. Speak slower, please. (for.)   *Hable más despacio, por favor.*
    <u>Ah</u>-bleh mahss dess-<u>pah</u>-see-oh, por fah-<u>vor</u>

96. What does . . . mean?   *¿Qué significa . . . ?*
    Keh seeg-nee-<u>fee</u>-kah

97. What does this say?   *¿Qué dice aquí?*   Keh <u>dee</u>-seh ah-<u>kee</u>

98. How do you say . . . in Spanish?
    ¿Cómo se dice . . . en español?
    <u>Koh</u>-moh seh <u>dee</u>-seh . . . en ess-pah-<u>nyohl</u>

99. How do you pronounce this word?
    ¿Cómo se pronuncia esta palabra?
    <u>Koh</u>-moh seh proh-<u>noon</u>-see-ah <u>ess</u>-tah pah-<u>lah</u>-brah

100. Can you translate it for me? (for./inf.)
     ¿Me lo puede(s) traducir?
     Meh loh <u>pweh</u>-deh(dess) trah-doo-<u>seer</u>

101. Can you write it down? (for./inf.)   *¿Puede(s) escribirlo?*
     <u>Pweh</u>-deh(dess) es-kree-<u>beer</u>-loh

102. How do you spell it?   *¿Cómo se deletrea?*
     <u>Koh</u>-moh seh deh-leh-<u>treh</u>-ah

103. Do you have a dictionary? (for./inf.)
     ¿Tiene(s) un diccionario?
     Tee-<u>eh</u>-neh (nehss) oon deek-see-oh-<u>nah</u>-ree-oh

104. That's not what I meant.   *Eso no es lo que quise decir.*
     <u>Eh</u>-soh noh ess loh keh <u>kee</u>-seh deh-<u>seer</u>

105. What I wanted to say was . . .   *Lo que quería decir es . . .*
     Loh keh keh-<u>ree</u>-ah deh-<u>seer</u> ess

THE BASICS

106. I have a problem.   *Tengo un problema.*
     <u>Ten</u>-goh oon proh-<u>bleh</u>-mah

107. I am lost. (m./f.)   *Estoy perdido/a.*
     Ess-<u>toy</u> pehr-<u>dee</u>-doh/ah

108. I don't know where I am.   *No sé dónde estoy.*
     Noh seh <u>dohn</u>-deh ess-<u>toy</u>

109. Help me, please. (for.)   *Ayúdeme, por favor.*
     Ah-<u>yoo</u>-deh-meh, por fah-<u>vor</u>

110.   Can you help me? (for./inf.)   *¿Me puede(s) ayudar?*
Meh <u>pweh</u>-deh(s) ah-yoo-<u>dar</u>

111.   Who can help me?   *¿Quién me puede ayudar?*
Kee-en meh <u>pweh</u>-deh ah-yoo-<u>dar</u>

112.   Who can I ask?   *¿A quién le puedo preguntar?*
Ah kee-<u>en</u> leh <u>pweh</u>-doh preh-goon-<u>tar</u>

113.   I need help.   *Necesito ayuda.*   Neh-seh-<u>see</u>-toh ah-<u>yoo</u>-dah
   . . . information.   . . . *información.*   een-for-mah-see-<u>ohn</u>
   . . . a city map.   . . . *un mapa de la ciudad.*
oon <u>mah</u>-pah deh lah <u>see</u>-oo-dahd
   . . . money.   . . . *dinero.*   dee-<u>neh</u>-roh
   . . . food.   . . . *comida.*   koh-<u>mee</u>-dah

114.   I'm looking for something to eat/drink.
Estoy buscando algo de comer/beber.
Ess-<u>toy</u> boos-<u>kahn</u>-doh <u>ahl</u>-goh deh koh-<u>mehr</u>/beh-<u>behr</u>

115.   Where is there a restroom?
¿Dónde hay un baño/ unos servicios? (Sp.)
<u>Dohn</u>-deh I oon <u>bah</u>-nyoh/<u>oo</u>-nohss sehr-<u>vee</u>-see-ohss

116.   Can I make a phone call?
¿Puedo hacer una llamada (telefónica)?
<u>Pweh</u>-doh ah-<u>sehr</u> <u>oo</u>-nah yah-<u>mah</u>-dah (teh-leh-<u>foh</u>-nee-kah)

117.   I need to go to the (U.S.) consulate/the embassy.
Necesito ir al consulado/a la embajada (de Estados Unidos).
Neh-seh-<u>see</u>-toh eer ahl kohn-sool-<u>ah</u>-doh/ah lah
em-bah-<u>hah</u>-dah deh Ess-<u>tah</u>-dohss Oo-<u>nee</u>-dohss

118.   Can I use the phone?   *¿Puedo usar el teléfono?*
<u>Pweh</u>-doh oo-<u>sar</u> el teh-<u>leh</u>-foh-noh
   . . . the restroom?   . . . *el baño/los servicios? (Sp.)*
el <u>bah</u>-nyoh/lohss sehr-<u>vee</u>-see-ohss

119.   It's urgent.   *Es urgente.*   Ess oor-<u>hen</u>-teh

120.   Where is the train station?
¿Dónde está la estación de tren?
<u>Dohn</u>-deh ess-<u>tah</u> lah ess-tah-see-<u>ohn</u> deh tren

. . . police station? . . . *de policía?* **deh poh-lee-_see_-ah**

. . . bus station? . . . *de autobús?* **deh ow-toh-_boos_**

121. Please take me to . . . *Por favor lléveme a . . .*
Por fah-_vor_ _yeh_-veh-meh ah

. . . the airport. . . . *al aeropuerto.* **ahl I-roh-_pwehr_-toh**

122. I want to go downtown. *Quiero ir al centro.*
Kee-_eh_-roh eer ahl _sen_-troh

. . . to this address. . . . *a esta dirección.*
ah _ess_-tah dee-rek-see-_ohn_

123. I want to go back home. *Quiero regresar a casa.*
Kee-_eh_-roh reh-greh-_sar_ ah _kah_-sah

. . . to the hotel. . . . *al hotel.* **ahl oh-_tel_**

124. Where can I find a drugstore?
¿Dónde puedo encontrar una farmacia?
Dohn-deh _pweh_-doh en-kohn-_trar_ _oo_-nah far-_mah_-see-ah

. . . a supermarket? . . . *un supermercado?*
oon _soo_-pehr mehr-_kah_-doh

. . . a travel agency? . . . *una agencia de viajes?*
_oo_-nah ah-_hen_-see-ah deh vee-_ah_-hess

125. What is this/that? *¿Qué es esto/eso?*
Keh ess _ess_-toh/_eh_-soh

126. Who is he/she? *¿Quién es él/ella?* **Kee-_en_ ess el/_eh_-yah**

127. When do we eat? *¿Cuándo comemos?*
Kwahn-doh koh-_meh_-mohss

128. What can we eat? *¿Qué podemos comer?*
Keh poh-_deh_-mohss koh-_mehr_

129. Where are we? *¿Dónde estamos?*
Dohn-deh ess-_tah_-mohss

130. Where are we going? *¿A dónde vamos?*
Ah _dohn_-deh _vah_-mohss

131. How can we get to . . . ? *¿Cómo podemos llegar a . . . ?*
Koh-moh poh-_deh_-mohss yeh-_gar_ ah

132. What for?   *¿Para qué?*   <u>Pah</u>-rah keh

133. Why (not)?   *¿Por qué (no)?*   Por keh (noh)

134. I won't.   *No quiero.*   Noh kee-<u>eh</u>-roh

135. I can't.   *No puedo.*   Noh <u>pweh</u>-doh

136. Enough already!   *¡Basta!*   <u>Bahss</u>-tah

PERSONAL PORTRAITS & EMOTIONS

137. Can you describe the person?
      ¿Puede describir a la persona?
      <u>Pweh</u>-deh dess-kree-<u>beer</u> ah lah pehr-<u>soh</u>-nah

138. What does he/she look like?   *¿Cómo es?*
      <u>Koh</u>-moh ess

139. How old is he/she?   *¿Cuántos años tiene?*
      <u>Kwahn</u>-tohss <u>ah</u>-nyohss tee-<u>eh</u>-neh

140. He/she is young/old.   *Es joven/viejo.*
      Ess <u>hoh</u>-vehn/vee-<u>eh</u>-hoh

      . . . a child.   *. . . un niño/a.*   oon <u>nee</u>-nyoh/ah

141. What's his/her weight?   *¿Cuánto pesa?*
      <u>Kwahn</u>-toh <u>peh</u>-sah

142. He/she weighs around 180/130 pounds.
      Pesa más o menos ochenta/sesenta kilos.
      <u>Peh</u>-sah mahss oh <u>meh</u>-nohss oh-<u>chen</u>-tah/
      seh-<u>sen</u>-tah <u>kee</u>-lohss

143. What is his/her height?   *¿Cuánto mide?*
      <u>Kwahn</u>-toh <u>mee</u>-deh

144. He/she is 6/5 feet tall.   *Mide un metro ochenta/cincuenta.*
      <u>Mee</u>-deh oon <u>meh</u>-troh oh-<u>chen</u>-tah/seen-<u>kwen</u>-tah

145. What does he/she look like?   *¿Cómo es?*   <u>Koh</u>-moh ess

146. He/she has short/long hair.   *Tiene el pelo corto/largo.*
      Tee-<u>eh</u>-neh el <u>peh</u>-loh <u>kor</u>-toh/<u>lar</u>-goh

. . . straight/curly.   . . . *lacio/rizado.*
lah-see-oh/ree-sah-doh

. . . light/dark.   . . . *claro/oscuro.*   **klah-roh/ohss-koo-roh**

147. He/she is bald.   *Es calvo/a.*   Ess **cahl-voh/ah**

148. He/she has fair/dark skin.   *Tiene la piel clara/oscura.*
Tee-eh-neh lah pee-el klah-rah/ohss-koo-rah

. . . pale.   . . . *pálida.*   **pah-lee-dah**

149. He/she has light/dark colored eyes.
Tiene los ojos claros/oscuros.
Tee-eh-neh lohss oh-hohss klah-rohss/ohss-koo-rohss

150. He wears a moustache/beard.   *Lleva bigote/barba.*
Yeh-vah bee-goh-teh/bar-bah

151. He/she is (very) fat.   *Es (muy) gordo/a.*
Ess (mooy) gor-doh/ah

. . . thin. (m./f.)   . . . *flaco/a.*   **flah-koh/ah**

. . . short. (m./f.)   . . . *bajo/a.*   **bah-hoh/ah**

. . . tall. (m./f.)   . . . *alto/a.*   **ahl-toh/ah**

152. He/she has a tattoo.   *Tiene un tatuaje.*
Tee-eh-neh oon tah-twah-heh

. . . a piercing.   . . . *un pirsin.*   **oon peer-seen**

153. He is very ugly/handsome.   *Es muy feo/guapo.*
Ess (mooy) feh-oh/gwah-poh

154. She is very ugly/beautiful.   *Es muy fea/bella.*
Ess (mooy) feh-ah/beh-yah

155. He/she is a (very) happy/serious person.
Es una persona (muy) alegre/seria.
Ess oo-nah pehr-soh-nah (mooy) ah-leh-greh/seh-ree-ah

. . . a (very) funny person.   . . . *(muy) chistosa.*
(mooy) chees-toh-sah

. . . a (very) intelligent person.   . . . *(muy) inteligente.*
(mooy) een-teh-lee-hen-teh

156. He's a great guy.   *Es un gran tipo.*   **Ess oon grahn tee-poh**

157. He/she has a (great) sense of humor.
Tiene un (gran) sentido del humor.
Tee-<u>eh</u>-neh oon (grahn) sen-<u>tee</u>-doh del oo <u>mohr</u>

158. He/she makes me laugh.   *Me hace reír.*
Meh <u>ah</u>-seh reh-<u>eer</u>

159. He/she thinks he's so smart.   *Se cree muy listo/a.*
Seh kreh mooy <u>lees</u>-toh/-tah

160. In fact, he/she's (very) dumb.   *En realidad es (muy) tonto/a*
En reh-ah-lee-<u>dahd</u> es (mooy) <u>ton</u>-toh/-tah

161. I like him/her (a lot).   *Me cae (muy) bien.*
Meh <u>kah</u>-eh (mooy) bee-<u>en</u>

162. I love him/her (a lot).   *Lo/la quiero (mucho).*
Loh/lah kee-<u>eh</u>-roh (<u>moo</u>-choh)

163. I dislike him/her (a lot).   *Me cae (muy) mal.*
Meh <u>kah</u>-eh (mooy) mahl

164. I can't stand him/her.   *No lo/la soporto.*
Noh loh/lah soh-<u>por</u>-toh

165. I detest him/her.   *Lo/la detesto.*   Loh/lah deh-<u>tess</u>-toh

166. I hate him/her.   *Lo/la odio.*   Loh/lah <u>oh</u>-dee-oh

167. He/she seems (very) happy/depressed.
Se le ve (muy) feliz/deprimido.
Seh leh veh (mooy) feh-<u>lees</u>/deh-pree-<u>mee</u>-doh

168. I feel (very) happy/sad.   *Me siento (muy) feliz/triste.*
Meh see-<u>en</u>-toh (mooy) feh-<u>lees</u>/<u>trees</u>-teh

169. I feel like crying.   *Tengo ganas de llorar.*
<u>Ten</u>-goh <u>gah</u>-nahss deh yoh-<u>rar</u>

170. I'm (very) angry.   *Estoy (muy) enojado.*
Ess-<u>toy</u> (mooy) eh-noh-<u>hah</u>-doh

171. I'm (very) scared.   *Tengo (mucho) miedo.*
<u>Ten</u>-goh (<u>moo</u>-choh) mee-<u>eh</u>-doh

172. You're scaring me. *Me estás asustando.*
Meh ess-<u>tahss</u> ah-soos-<u>tahn</u>-doh

DATE & TIME

173. What day is today? *¿Qué día es (hoy)?*
Keh <u>dee</u>-ah ess (oy)

174. Today is Monday. *Hoy es lunes.* Oy ess <u>loo</u>-ness
. . . Tuesday. . . . *martes.* <u>mar</u>-tess
. . . Wednesday. . . . *miércoles.* mee-<u>ehr</u>-koh-less
. . . Thursday. . . . *jueves.* <u>hweh</u>-vess
. . . Friday. . . . *viernes.* vee-<u>ehr</u>-ness
. . . Saturday. . . . *sábado.* <u>sah</u>-bah-doh
. . . Sunday. . . . *domingo.* doh-<u>meen</u>-goh
. . . my birthday. . . . *mi cumpleaños.*
mee koom-pleh-<u>ah</u>-nyohss

175. What day is tomorrow/the day after tomorrow?
¿Qué día es mañana/pasado mañana?
Keh <u>dee</u>-ah ess mah-<u>nyah</u>-nah/pah-<u>sah</u>-doh mah-<u>nyah</u>-nah

176. What day was yesterday? *¿Qué día fue ayer?*
Keh <u>dee</u>-ah foo-<u>eh</u> ah-<u>yehr</u>

177. What are you all doing tonight?
¿Qué van a hacer esta noche?
Keh vahn ah ah-<u>sehr</u> <u>ess</u>-tah <u>noh</u>-cheh

178. What did you do last night? *¿Qué hiciste anoche?*
Keh ee-<u>sees</u>-teh ah-<u>noh</u>-cheh

179. What month are we in? *¿En qué mes estamos?*
En keh mess ess-<u>tah</u>-mohss

180. It's January. *Es el mes de enero.*
Ess el mess deh eh-<u>neh</u>-roh
. . . February. . . . *febrero.* feh-<u>breh</u>-roh
. . . March. . . . *marzo.* <u>mar</u>-soh
. . . April. . . . *abril.* ah-<u>breel</u>

. . . May.	. . . *mayo.*	**mah**-yoh
. . . June.	. . . *junio.*	**hoo**-nee-oh
. . . July.	. . . *julio.*	**hoo**-lee-oh
. . . August.	. . . *agosto.*	ah-**gohs**-toh
. . . September.	. . . *septiembre.*	sep-tee-**em**-breh
. . . October.	. . . *octubre.*	ohk-**too**-breh
. . . November.	. . . *noviembre.*	noh-vee-**em**-breh
. . . December.	. . . *diciembre.*	dee-see-**em**-breh

181. What's the date?   *¿Cuál es la fecha?*
Kwahl ess lah **feh**-chah

182. Today is Monday, January first.
Hoy es lunes primero de enero.
Oy ess **loo**-ness pree-**meh**-roh deh eh-**neh**-roh

183. Next year I'm going to travel through Spain.
El año próximo voy a viajar por España.
El **ah**-nyoh **prohk**-see-moh voy ah vee-ah-**har** por
Ess-**pah**-nyah

184. Last year I went to Mexico.   *El año pasado fui a México.*
El **ah**-nyoh pah-**sah**-doh **fwee** ah **Meh**-hee-koh

185. I will go to Peru in the spring.   *Iré a Perú en la primavera.*
Eer-**eh** ah Peh-**roo** en lah pree-mah-**veh**-rah

186. What are your plans for the summer? (inf.)
¿Qué planes tienes para el verano?
Keh **plah**-ness tee-**eh**-ness **pah**-rah el veh-**rah**-noh

187. I love the fall.   *Me encanta el otoño.*
Meh en-**kahn**-tah el oh-**toh**-nyoh

188. It's cold in the winter.   *Hace frío en el invierno.*
Ah-seh **free**-oh en el een-vee-**ehr**-noh

189. To every thing there is a season.   *Hay un tiempo para todo.*
I oon tee-**em**-poh **pah**-rah **toh**-doh

190. Do you have a watch? (inf.)   *¿Tienes un reloj?*
Tee-**eh**-ness oon reh-**lohh**

191. What time is it? *¿Qué hora es?* Keh <u>oh</u>-rah ess

192. It's one/It's two o'clock in the morning.
Es la una/Son las dos de la mañana.
Ess la <u>oo</u>-nah/Sohn lahss dohss deh lah mah-<u>nyah</u>-nah

   . . . in the afternoon/evening. . . . *de la tarde.*
   deh lah <u>tar</u>-deh

193. It's eight o'clock at night. *Son las ocho de la noche.*
Sohn lahss <u>oh</u>-choh deh lah <u>noh</u>-cheh

194. It's nine-twenty. *Son las nueve y veinte.*
Sohn lahss <u>nweh</u>-veh ee <u>vayn</u>-teh

195. It's a quarter past ten. *Son las diez y cuarto.*
Sohn lahss dee-<u>ess</u> ee <u>kwar</u>-toh

196. It's half past twelve. *Son las doce y media.*
Sohn lahss <u>doh</u>-seh ee <u>meh</u>-dee-ah

197. It's a quarter to eleven.
Es un cuarto para las once/las once menos cuarto.
Ess oon <u>kwar</u>-toh <u>pah</u>-rah lahss <u>on</u>-seh/lahss <u>on</u>-seh
<u>meh</u>-nohss <u>kwar</u>-toh

198. I think that clock is slow/fast.
Creo que ese reloj está atrasado/adelantado.
<u>Kreh</u>-oh keh <u>ess</u>-eh reh-<u>lohh</u> ess-tah ah-trah-<u>sah</u>-doh/
ah-deh-lahn-<u>tah</u>-doh

199. At what time . . . ? At three. *¿A qué hora . . . ? A las tres.*
Ah keh <u>oh</u>-rah . . . Ah lahss trehss

200. It's (very) early/late. *Es (muy) temprano/tarde.*
Ess (mooy) tem-<u>prah</u>-noh/<u>tar</u>-deh

201. What a beautiful sunset! *¡Qué bonito atardecer!*
Keh boh-<u>nee</u>-toh ah-tar-deh-<u>sehr</u>

202. It's only dusk/dawn. *Apenas es el anochecer/amanecer.*
Ah-<u>peh</u>-nahss ess el ah-noh-cheh-<u>sehr</u>/ah-mah-neh-<u>sehr</u>

203. It's already noon/midnight. *Ya es mediodía/medianoche.*
Yah ess meh-dee-oh-<u>dee</u>-ah/meh-dee-ah-<u>noh</u>-cheh

204. I need to wake up at . . .   *Necesito despertarme a las . . .*
     Neh-seh-<u>see</u>-toh dess-pehr-<u>tar</u>-meh ah lahss

205. I must leave at . . . at the latest.
     Debo salir a más tardar a las . . .
     <u>Deh</u>-boh sah-<u>leer</u> ah mahss tar-<u>dar</u> ah lahss

206. I have to leave in a few minutes.
     Me tengo que ir dentro de unos minutos.
     Meh <u>ten</u>-goh keh eer <u>den</u>-troh deh <u>oo</u>-nohss mee-<u>noo</u>-tohss

207. I want to get there early.   *Quiero llegar temprano.*
     Kee-<u>eh</u>-roh yeh-<u>gar</u> tem-<u>prah</u>-noh

208. I don't have time to . . .   *No tengo tiempo de . . .*
     Noh <u>ten</u>-goh tee-<u>em</u>-poh deh

209. I'm in a (big) hurry.   *Tengo (mucha) prisa.*
     <u>Ten</u>-goh (<u>moo</u>-chah) <u>pree</u>-sah

210. We're never going to get there at this pace.
     Nunca vamos a llegar a este paso.
     <u>Noon</u>-kah <u>vah</u>-mohss ah yeh-<u>gar</u> ah <u>ess</u>-teh <u>pah</u>-soh

211. Hurry up. (for.)   *Dese prisa/apresúrese/apúrese.*
     <u>Deh</u>-seh <u>pree</u>-sah/ah-preh-<u>soo</u>-reh-seh/ah-<u>poo</u>-reh-seh

     Hurry up. (inf.)   *Date prisa/apresúrate/apúrate.*
     <u>Dah</u>-teh <u>pree</u>-sah/ah-preh-<u>soo</u>-rah-teh/ah-<u>poo</u>-rah-teh

212. Let's go!   *¡Vamos!*   <u>Vah</u>-mohss

213. Fast!   *¡Rápido!*   <u>Rah</u>-pee-doh

214. I can't go any faster.   *No puedo ir más rápido.*
     Noh <u>pweh</u>-doh eer mahss <u>rah</u>-pee-doh

215. We're running late.   *Vamos retrasados.*
     <u>Vah</u>-mohss reh-trah-<u>sah</u>-dohss

216. We're going to be late.   *Vamos a llegar tarde.*
     <u>Vah</u>-mohss ah yeh-<u>gar</u> <u>tar</u>-deh

217. How much longer do we have?   *¿Cuánto tiempo nos queda?*
     <u>Kwahn</u>-toh tee-<u>em</u>-poh nohss <u>keh</u>-dah

218. It's too late.   *Es demasiado tarde.*
Ess deh-mah-see-<u>ah</u>-doh <u>tar</u>-deh

219. It's been a while since . . .   *Hace mucho (tiempo) que no . . .*
<u>Ah</u>-seh <u>moo</u>-choh (tee-<u>em</u>-poh) keh noh

220. Let's go next week.   *Vamos la semana próxima.*
<u>Vah</u>-mohss lah seh-<u>mah</u>-nah <u>prohk</u>-see-mah

221. Time flies.   *El tiempo vuela.*   **El tee-<u>em</u>-poh <u>vweh</u>-lah**

CELEBRATIONS

222. When is your birthday?   *¿Cuándo es tu cumpleaños?*
<u>Kwahn</u>-doh ess too koom-pleh-<u>ah</u>-nyohss

223. Today is my birthday.   *Hoy es mi cumpleaños.*
Oy ess mee koom-pleh-<u>ah</u>-nyohss

224. Happy birthday!   *¡Feliz cumpleaños!*
Feh-<u>lees</u> koom-pleh-<u>ah</u>-nyohss

225. Many happy returns!   *¡Felicidades!*   **Feh-lee-see-<u>dah</u>-dess**

226. Congratulations!   *¡Felicitaciones!*
Feh-lee-see-tah-see-<u>oh</u>-ness

227. How old are you?   *¿Cuántos años cumples?*
<u>Kwahn</u>-tohss <u>ah</u>-nyohss <u>koom</u>-pless

228. What do you want as a present?   *¿Qué quieres de regalo?*
Keh kee-<u>eh</u>-ress deh reh-<u>gah</u>-loh

229. Let's go celebrate.   *Vamos a festejar.*
<u>Vah</u>-mohss ah fess-teh-<u>hahr</u>

230. We just got married.   *Nos acabamos de casar.*
Nohss ah-kah-<u>bah</u>-mohss deh kah-<u>sar</u>

231. We're having a baby.   *Vamos a tener un bebé.*
<u>Vah</u>-mohss ah teh-<u>nehr</u> oon beh-<u>beh</u>

232. Congratulations!   *¡Enhorabuena!*   **En-oh-rah-<u>bweh</u>-nah**

233. What holidays do you celebrate here?
     ¿Qué fiestas celebran aquí?
     Keh fee-<u>ess</u>-tahss seh-<u>leh</u>-brahn ah-<u>kee</u>

234. How are they celebrated?   *¿Cómo se celebran?*
     <u>Koh</u>-moh seh seh-<u>leh</u>-brahn

235. When is Independence Day?
     ¿Cuándo es el día de la independencia? (L. Am.)
     <u>Kwahn</u>-doh ess el <u>dee</u>-ah deh lah een-deh-pen-<u>den</u>-see-ah

236. When does Mardi Gras begin?
     ¿Cuándo empieza el carnaval?
     <u>Kwahn</u>-doh em-pee-<u>eh</u>-sah el kar-nah-<u>vahl</u>

237. When are the next holidays?
     ¿Cuándo son las próximas vacaciones?
     <u>Kwahn</u>-doh sohn lahss <u>prohk</u>-see-mahss vah-kah-see-<u>oh</u>-ness

238. Tonight is Christmas Eve.   *Esta noche es Noche Buena.*
     <u>Ess</u>-tah <u>noh</u>-cheh ess <u>noh</u>-cheh <u>bweh</u>-nah

239. Tomorrow is Christmas.   *Mañana es Navidad.*
     Mah-<u>nyah</u>-nah ess nah-vee-<u>dahd</u>

240. Merry Christmas!   *¡Feliz Navidad!*   Feh-<u>lees</u> nah-vee-<u>dahd</u>

241. Prosperous New Year!   *¡Próspero año nuevo!*
     <u>Prohss</u>-peh-roh <u>ah</u>-nyoh <u>nweh</u>-voh

242. Happy holidays!   *¡Felices fiestas!*
     Feh-<u>lee</u>-sess fee-<u>ess</u>-tahss

THE WEATHER

243. How's the weather?   *¿Cómo está el clima?*
     <u>Koh</u>-moh ess-<u>tah</u> el <u>klee</u>-mah

244. The weather's good/bad.   *Hace buen/mal clima.*
     <u>Ah</u>-seh bwen/mahl <u>klee</u>-mah

245. It's (very) cloudy/sunny.   *Está (muy) nublado/soleado.*
     Ess-<u>tah</u> (mooy) noo-<u>blah</u>-doh/soh-leh-<u>ah</u>-doh
        . . . dry/humid.   . . . *seco/húmedo.*   <u>seh</u>-koh/<u>oo</u>-meh-doh

246. What's the temperature?   ¿Cuál es la temperatura?
Kwahl ess lah tem-peh-rah-<u>too</u>-rah

247. It's (very) hot/cold.   Hace (mucho) calor/frío.
<u>Ah</u>-seh (<u>moo</u>-choh) kah-<u>lor</u>/<u>free</u>-oh

. . . windy.   . . . viento.   vee-<u>en</u>-toh

248. Do I need a sweater?   ¿Necesito un suéter?
Neh-seh-<u>see</u>-toh oon <u>sweh</u>-tehr

. . . a jacket?   . . . una chamarra? (L. Am.)
<u>oo</u>-nah chah-<u>mar</u>-rah

249. Should I take a short-sleeved shirt?
Debo llevar una camisa de manga corta?
<u>Deh</u>-boh yeh-<u>var</u> <u>oo</u>-nah kah-<u>mee</u>-sah deh <u>mahn</u>-gah <u>kor</u>-tah

. . . a T-shirt?   . . . una camiseta?
<u>oo</u>-nah kah-mee-<u>seh</u>-tah

250. It hasn't rained for a while.   Hace tiempo que no llueve.
<u>Ah</u>-seh tee-<u>em</u>-poh keh noh <u>yweh</u>-veh.

251. It looks like it's going to rain.
Parece que va a llover.   Pah-<u>reh</u>-seh keh vah ah yoh-<u>vehr</u>

252. The sky is getting cloudy.   El cielo se está nublando.
El see-<u>eh</u>-loh seh ess-<u>tah</u> noo-<u>blahn</u>-doh

253. It's (not) the rainy season.   (No) Es temporada de lluvias.
(Noh) Ess tem-poh-<u>rah</u>-dah deh <u>yoo</u>-vee-ahss

254. Should I take an umbrella?   ¿Debo llevar un paraguas?
<u>Deh</u>-boh yeh-<u>var</u> oon par-<u>ah</u>-wahss

255. It's raining.   Está lloviendo.   Ess-<u>tah</u> yoh-vee-<u>en</u>-doh

256. It's just drizzle.   Es sólo una llovizna.
Ess <u>soh</u>-loh <u>oo</u>-nah yoh-<u>vees</u>-nah

257. A storm is approaching.   Se acerca una tormenta.
Seh ah-<u>sehr</u>-kah <u>oo</u>-nah tor-<u>men</u>-tah

258. A thunderstorm?   ¿Una tormenta eléctrica?
Oo-nah tor-<u>men</u>-tah eh-<u>lek</u>-tree-kah

259. It's raining by the bucketful.   *Está lloviendo a cántaros.*
Ess-<u>tah</u> yoh-vee-<u>en</u>-doh ah <u>kahn</u>-tah-rohss

260. There's thunder and lightning.   *Hay rayos y truenos.*
I <u>rah</u>-yohss ee <u>trweh</u>-nohss

261. When will the sun shine again?
¿Cuándo saldrá otra vez el sol?
<u>Kwahn</u>-doh sahl-<u>drah</u> <u>oh</u>-trah vess el sohl

262. Tomorrow will be clear/rainy/stormy.
Mañana estará despejado/lluvioso/tormentoso.
Mah-<u>nyah</u>-nah ess-tah-<u>rah</u> dess-peh-<u>hah</u>-doh/
yoo-vee-<u>ohss</u>-oh/tor-men-<u>toh</u>-soh

263. I love this weather!   *¡Me encanta este clima!*
Meh en-<u>kahn</u>-tah <u>ess</u>-teh <u>klee</u>-mah

264. I hate this weather!   *¡Odio este clima!*
<u>Oh</u>-dee-oh <u>ess</u>-teh <u>klee</u>-mah

265. I can't control the weather.   *No puedo controlar el clima.*
Noh <u>pweh</u>-doh kohn-troh-<u>lahr</u> el <u>klee</u>-mah

GETTING THERE

266. Where is the airport?   *¿Dónde está el aeropuerto?*
<u>Dohn</u>-deh ess-<u>tah</u> el I-roh-<u>pwehr</u>-toh

. . . the train station?   *. . . la estación del tren?*
lah ess-tah-see-<u>ohn</u> del tren

267. Are we near/far from the port?
¿Estamos cerca/lejos del puerto?
Ess-<u>tah</u>-mohss <u>sehr</u>-kah/<u>leh</u>-hohss del <u>pwehr</u>-toh

. . . the bus stop/terminal?
. . . de la parada/terminal de autobuses?
deh lah pah-<u>rah</u>-dah /tehr-mee-<u>nahl</u> deh ow-toh-<u>boo</u>-sess

268. At what time does the flight to . . . leave?
¿A qué hora sale el vuelo a . . . ?
Ah keh <u>oh</u>-rah <u>sah</u>-leh el <u>vweh</u>-loh ah

. . . the train to . . . leave?   *. . . el tren a . . . ?*   el tren ah

. . . the bus to . . . leave?   . . . *el autobús a . . . ?*
el ow-toh-<u>boos</u> ah

. . . the boat to . . . leave?   . . . *el barco a . . . ?*
el <u>bar</u>-koh ah

269. I need to take the next flight to . . .
      Necesito tomar el próximo vuelo a . . .
      Neh-seh-<u>see</u>-toh toh-<u>mahr</u> el <u>prohk</u>-see-moh <u>vweh</u>-loh ah

      . . . the first/last flight to . . .
      . . . *el primer/último vuelo a . . .*
      el pree-<u>mehr</u>/<u>ool</u>-tee-moh <u>vweh</u>-loh ah

270. We can't miss that boat!   *¡No podemos perder ese barco!*
      Noh poh-<u>deh</u>-mohss pehr-<u>dehr</u> <u>eh</u>-seh <u>bar</u>-koh

271. I think we missed the train.   *Creo que perdimos el tren.*
      <u>Kreh</u>-oh keh pehr-<u>dee</u>-mohss el tren

272. At what time does the flight coming from . . . arrive?
      ¿A qué hora llega el vuelo que viene de . . . ?
      Ah keh <u>oh</u>-rah <u>yeh</u>-gah el <u>vweh</u>-loh keh vee-<u>eh</u>-neh deh

273. Do you have the arrival/departure schedule? (for.)
      ¿Tiene el horario de salidas/llegadas?
      Tee-<u>eh</u>-neh el oh-<u>rah</u>-ree-oh deh sahl-<u>ee</u>-dahss/yeh-<u>gah</u>-dahss

274. Where is the ticket counter?   *¿Dónde está la taquilla?*
      <u>Dohn</u>-deh ess-<u>tah</u> lah tah-<u>kee</u>-yah

      . . . the waiting area?   . . . *la sala de espera?*
      lah <u>sah</u>-lah deh ess-<u>peh</u>-rah

      . . . the departure gate?   . . . *la puerta de embarque?*
      lah <u>pwehr</u>-tah deh em-<u>bar</u>-keh

275. What's the train platform number?
      ¿Cuál es el número del andén?
      Kwahl ess el <u>noo</u>-meh-roh del ahn-<u>den</u>

      . . . the dock number?   . . . *el número del muelle?*
      el <u>noo</u>-meh-roh del <u>mweh</u>-yeh

276. How much is a ticket to . . . ?
      ¿Cuánto cuesta el boleto a . . . ?
      <u>Kwahn</u>-toh <u>kwess</u>-tah el boh-<u>leh</u>-toh ah

... a ticket to ...?   ... *el billete a ...? (Sp.)*
el bee-<u>yeh</u>-teh ah

277.   Is it a direct trip?   *¿Es un viaje directo?*
Ess oon vee-<u>ah</u>-heh dee-<u>rek</u>-toh

278.   How many stops/transfers are there?
¿Cuántas paradas/cuántos cambios hay?
<u>Kwahn</u>-tahss pah-<u>rah</u>-das/<u>kwahn</u>-tohss <u>kahm</u>-bee-ohss I

279.   How long does it take to get to ...?
¿Cuánto tarda en llegar a ...?
<u>Kwahn</u>-toh <u>tar</u>-dah en yeh-<u>gar</u> ah

280.   Is there a discount for students?
¿Hay descuento para estudiantes?
I dess-<u>kwen</u>-toh <u>pah</u>-rah ess-too-dee-<u>ahn</u>-tess

... for teachers?   ... *para profesores?*
<u>pah</u>-rah proh-feh-<u>soh</u>-ress

... for the elderly?   ... *para personas mayores?*
<u>pah</u>-rah pehr-<u>sohn</u>-ahss mah-<u>yoh</u>-ress

281.   Does it include travelers' insurance?
¿Incluye seguro de viajero?
Een-<u>kloo</u>-yeh seh-<u>goo</u>-roh deh vee-ah-<u>heh</u>-roh

282.   I want a round trip ticket.
Quiero un boleto/billete de ida y vuelta.
Kee-<u>eh</u>-roh oon boh-<u>leh</u>-toh/bee-<u>yeh</u>-teh de <u>ee</u>-dah ee <u>vwel</u>-tah

... a one-way ticket.   ... *de ida solamente.*
deh <u>ee</u>-dah soh-lah-<u>men</u>-teh

283.   Give me a first-class ticket.
Deme un boleto/billete de primera clase.
<u>Deh</u>-meh oon boh-<u>leh</u>-toh/bee-<u>yeh</u>-teh deh pree-<u>meh</u>-rah
<u>klah</u>-seh

... an economy ticket.   ... *de clase económica.*
deh <u>klah</u>-seh eh-koh-<u>noh</u>-mee-kah

284.   I would like a seat in the smoking/non-smoking section.
Me gustaría un asiento en la sección de fumar/de no fumar.
Meh goos-tah-<u>ree</u>-ah oon ah-see-<u>en</u>-toh en lah sek-see-<u>ohn</u> deh
foo-<u>mar</u>/deh noh foo-<u>mar</u>

285. I prefer a window seat.   *Prefiero un asiento con ventanilla.*
Preh-fee-**eh**-roh oon ah-see-**en**-toh kohn ven-tah-**nee**-yah

   . . . an aisle seat.   . . . *en el pasillo.*   en el pahss-**see**-yoh

286. Do I need to make a reservation?
¿Necesito hacer una reservación?
Neh-seh-**see**-toh ah-**sehr** **oo**-nah reh-sehr-vah-see-**ohn**

287. I want to reserve a seat/two seats.
Quiero reservar un asiento/dos asientos.
Kee-**eh**-roh reh-sehr-**var** oon ah-see-**en**-toh/dohss
ah-see-**en**-tohss

288. Does it leave on time?   *¿Sale puntualmente?*
Sah-leh poon-twahl-**men**-teh

289. Is it on time/delayed?   *¿Está a tiempo/retrasado?*
Ess-**tah** ah tee-**em**-poh/reh-trah-**sah**-doh

290. At what time can we board?
¿A qué hora podemos abordar/embarcar?
Ah keh **oh**-rah poh-**deh**-mohss ah-bor-**dar**/em-bar-**kar**

291. Is this the train/bus that goes to . . . ?
¿Éste es el tren/autobús que va a . . . ?
Ess-teh ess el tren/ow-toh-**boos** keh vah ah

292. Is this seat free?   *¿Está libre este asiento?*
Ess-**tah** **lee**-breh **ess**-teh ahss-ee-**en**-toh

293. May I sit here?   *¿Me puedo sentar aquí?*
Meh **pweh**-doh sen-**tar** ah-**kee**

294. You are sitting in my seat. (for.)
Está usted sentado/-a en mi asiento.
Ess-**tah** oo-**sted** sen-**tah**-doh/-ah en mee ah-see-**en**-toh

295. You are sitting in my seat. (inf.)
Estás sentado/-a en mi asiento.
Ess-**tahss** sen-**tah**-doh/-ah en mee ah-see-**en**-toh

296. That's my seat.   *Ése es mi asiento.*
Ess-eh ess mee ah-see-**en**-toh

297. Could you open the window (a little), please? (for.)
      ¿Podría abrir la ventanilla (un poco), por favor?
      Poh-<u>dree</u>-ah ah-<u>breer</u> lah ven-tah-<u>nee</u>-yah (oon <u>poh</u>-koh), por
      fah-<u>vor</u>

298. Do you mind if I open the window? (for.)
      ¿Le importa si abro la ventanilla?
      Leh eem-<u>por</u>-tah see <u>ah</u>-broh lah ven-tah-<u>nee</u>-yah

299. Have we arrived in . . . ?   *¿Ya llegamos a . . . ?*
      Yah yeh-<u>gah</u>-mohss ah

300. Should I get off here?   *¿Debo bajar aquí?*
      <u>Deh</u>-boh bah-<u>har</u> ah-<u>kee</u>

301. My luggage was damaged.   *Se dañó mi equipaje.*
      Seh dah-<u>nyoh</u> mee eh-kee-<u>pah</u>-heh

302. Where's my luggage?   *¿Dónde está mi equipaje?*
      <u>Dohn</u>-deh ess-<u>tah</u> mee eh-kee-<u>pah</u>-heh

303. I need to find my suitcase.   *Necesito encontrar mi maleta.*
      Neh-seh-<u>see</u>-toh en-kohn-<u>trar</u> mee mah-<u>leh</u>-tah

304. My luggage is missing/lost.   *Mi equipaje está perdido.*
      Mee eh-kee-<u>pah</u>-heh ess-<u>tah</u> pehr-<u>dee</u>-doh

305. My suitcase was stolen.   *Me robaron la maleta.*
      Meh roh-<u>bah</u>-rohn lah mah-<u>leh</u>-tah

306. Where can I buy a suitcase?
      ¿Dónde puedo comprar una maleta?
      <u>Dohn</u>-deh <u>pweh</u>-doh kohm-<u>prahr</u> <u>oo</u>-nah mah-<u>leh</u>-tah

GETTING ORIENTED

307. How do I get to . . . ?   *¿Cómo llego a . . . ?*
      <u>Koh</u>-moh <u>yeh</u>-goh ah

308. I want to go to . . .   *Quiero ir a . . .*   Kee-<u>eh</u>-roh eer ah

309. I'm looking for . . .   *Estoy buscando . . .*
      Ess-<u>toy</u> boos-<u>kahn</u>-doh

310. Do you know the address of . . . ?
¿Sabe la dirección de . . . ?
<u>Sah</u>-beh lah dee-rek-see-<u>ohn deh</u>

311. I need a (city/area) map.
Necesito un mapa (de la ciudad/del área).
Neh-seh-<u>see</u>-toh oon <u>mah</u>-pah (deh lah <u>see</u>-oo-dahd/del <u>ah</u>-reh-ah)

312. We need directions to get to . . .
Necesitamos direcciones para llegar a . . .
Neh-seh-see-<u>tah</u>-mohss dee-rek-see-<u>oh</u>-ness <u>pah</u>-rah yeh-<u>gahr</u> ah

313. How far is . . . ?   *¿Qué tan lejos está . . . ?*
Keh tahn <u>leh</u>-hohss ess-<u>tah</u>

314. Where is . . . ?   *¿Dónde está . . . ?*   <u>Dohn</u>-deh ess-<u>tah</u>

315. Where are we?   *¿Dónde estamos?*
<u>Dohn</u>-deh ess-<u>tah</u>-mohss

316. Can you show me on the map? (for.)
¿Puede señalarlo en el mapa?
<u>Pweh</u>-deh seh-nyah-<u>lar</u>-loh en el <u>mah</u>-pah

317. Should I keep going straight?   *¿Debo seguir derecho/recto?*
<u>Deh</u>-boh seh-<u>geer</u> deh-<u>reh</u>-choh/<u>rek</u>-toh

. . . go up to the square?   . . . *seguir hasta la plaza?*
seh-<u>geer</u> <u>ahss</u>-tah lah <u>plah</u>-sah

318. Do I turn right/left?   *¿Doy vuelta a la derecha/izquierda?*
Doy <u>vwel</u>-tah ah lah deh-<u>reh</u>-chah/ees-kee-<u>ehr</u>-dah

. . . turn at the corner?   . . . *en la esquina?*
en lah ess-<u>kee</u>-nah

. . . turn at the light?   . . . *en el semáforo?*
en el sem-<u>ah</u>-foh-roh

319. Do I need to go through the tunnel?
¿Necesito atravesar el túnel?
Neh-seh-<u>see</u>-toh ah-trah-veh-<u>sar</u> el <u>too</u>-nel

. . . go across the bridge?   . . . *cruzar por el puente?*
kroo-<u>sar</u> por el <u>pwen</u>-teh

320. Can you guide me there? (for.)   *¿Me puede guiar hasta allá?*
      Meh <u>pweh</u>-deh gee-<u>ahr</u> <u>ahss</u>-tah ah-<u>yah</u>

321. How many streets/city blocks are there left to go?
      ¿Cuántas calles/cuadras faltan?
      <u>Kwahn</u>-tahss <u>kah</u>-yess/<u>kwah</u>-drahss <u>fahl</u>-tahn

322. The store is in front of the museum.
      La tienda está frente al museo.
      Lah tee-<u>en</u>-dah ess-<u>tah</u> <u>fren</u>-teh ahl moo-<u>seh</u>-oh

      . . . behind the museum.   . . . *atrás/a espaldas del museo.*
      ah-<u>trahss</u>/ah ess-<u>pahl</u>-dahss del moo-<u>seh</u>-oh

      . . . next to the museum.   . . . *a un lado del museo.*
      ah oon <u>lah</u>-doh del moo-<u>seh</u>-oh

      . . . to the right of the museum.   . . . *a la derecha del museo.*
      ah lah deh-<u>reh</u>-chah del moo-<u>seh</u>-oh

      . . . to the left of the museum.
      . . . *a la izquierda del museo.*
      ah lah ees-kee-<u>ehr</u>-dah del moo-<u>seh</u>-oh

323. Is the museum near/far?   *¿Está cerca/lejos el museo?*
      Ess-<u>tah</u> <u>sehr</u>-kah/<u>leh</u>-hohss el moo-<u>seh</u>-oh

324. Can we walk there?   *¿Podemos caminar hasta allá?*
      Poh-<u>deh</u>-mohss kah-mee-<u>nahr</u> <u>ahss</u>-tah ah-<u>yah</u>

325. It's about ten minutes by foot.
      Son como diez minutos a pie.
      Sohn <u>koh</u>-moh dee-<u>ess</u> mee-<u>noo</u>-tohss ah pee-<u>eh</u>

326. Are we almost there?   *¿Ya casi llegamos?*
      Yah <u>kah</u>-see yeh-<u>gah</u>-mohss

GETTING AROUND

327. How can I get to . . . ?   *¿Cómo puedo llegar a . . . ?*
      <u>Koh</u>-moh <u>pweh</u>-doh yeh-<u>gar</u> ah

328. What's the best way to go to . . . ?
      ¿Cuál es la mejor manera de ir a . . . ?
      Kwahl ess lah meh-<u>hor</u> mah-<u>neh</u>-rah deh eer ah

329. Can you go on foot/walking?
¿Se puede ir a pie/caminando?
Seh <u>pweh</u>-deh eer ah pee-<u>eh</u>/kah-mee-<u>nahn</u>-doh

330. Can I get there by bus?   *¿Puedo llegar ahí en autobús?*
<u>Pweh</u>-doh yeh-<u>gar</u> ah-<u>ee</u> en ow-toh-<u>boos</u>

331. Is it complicated to go on the subway?
¿Es complicado ir en metro?
Ess kohm-plee-<u>kah</u>-doh eer en <u>meh</u>-troh

332. Is it better to take a taxi?   *¿Es mejor tomar un taxi?*
Ess meh-<u>hor</u> toh-<u>mar</u> oon <u>tah</u>-ksee

333. Where can I get a taxi?   *¿Dónde puedo conseguir un taxi?*
<u>Dohn</u>-deh <u>pweh</u>-doh kohn-seh-<u>geer</u> oon <u>tah</u>-ksee

334. Is it safe to take a taxi?   *¿Es seguro tomar un taxi?*
Ess seh-<u>goo</u>-roh toh-<u>mar</u> oon <u>tah</u>-ksee

335. Can you call a taxi for me? (for./inf.)
¿Puede(s) llamarme un taxi?
<u>Pweh</u>-deh(s) yah-<u>mar</u>-meh oon <u>tah</u>-ksee

336. I need a taxi at eight . . .   *Necesito un taxi a las ocho . . .*
Neh-seh-<u>see</u>-toh oon <u>tah</u>-ksee ah lahss <u>oh</u>-choh

337. Can you pick me up at . . . ? (for./inf.)
¿Puede(s) pasar por mí a las . . . ?
<u>Pweh</u>-deh(s) pah-<u>sar</u> por mee ah lahss

338. Are you available? (for.)   *¿Está libre?*   Ess-<u>tah</u> <u>lee</u>-breh

339. How much is it to go to the airport?
¿Cuánto cuesta ir al aeropuerto?
<u>Kwahn</u>-toh <u>kwess</u>-tah eer ahl I-roh-<u>pwehr</u>-toh
. . . to the hotel?   . . . *al hotel?*   ahl oh-<u>tel</u>
. . . to the downtown area?   . . . *al centro?*   ahl <u>sen</u>-troh
. . . to this address?   . . . *a esta dirección?*
ah <u>ess</u>-tah dee-rek-see-<u>ohn</u>

340. Do you charge by time or by distance?
¿Cobra por tiempo o por distancia?
<u>Koh</u>-brah por tee-<u>em</u>-poh oh por dees-<u>tahn</u>-see-ah

341. Is there an extra fee for the luggage?
 ¿Hay un cargo extra por las maletas?
 I oon <u>kar</u>-goh <u>eks</u>-trah por lahss mah-<u>leh</u> tahss

 . . . night service? . . . *servicio nocturno?*
 sehr-<u>vee</u>-see-oh nohk-<u>toor</u>-noh

 . . . more than three passengers? . . . *más de tres pasajeros?*
 mahss deh trehss pah-sah-<u>heh</u>-rohss

342. Please, take me to the train station. (for.)
 Por favor, lléveme a la estación de tren.
 Por fah-<u>vor</u>, <u>yeh</u>-veh-meh ah lah ess-tah-see-<u>ohn</u> deh tren

 . . . to the bus terminal. . . . *a la terminal de autobuses.*
 ah lah tehr-mee-<u>nahl</u> deh ow-toh-<u>boo</u>-sess

 . . . to the hospital. . . . *al hospital.* ahl ohss-pee-<u>tahl</u>

343. Is the meter working? *¿Funciona el taxímetro?*
 foon-see-<u>ohn</u>-ah el tahk-<u>see</u>-meh-troh

344. Drive slower/faster, please. (for.)
 Vaya más despacio/rápido, por favor.
 <u>Vah</u>-yah mahss dess-<u>pah</u>-see-oh/<u>rah</u>-pee-doh, por fah-<u>vor</u>

345. I'm (not) in a hurry. *(No) Tengo prisa.*
 (Noh) <u>Ten</u>-goh <u>pree</u>-sah

346. Stop at the corner. (for.) *Pare en la esquina.*
 <u>Pah</u>-reh en lah ess-<u>kee</u>-nah

347. Here is fine. *Aquí está bien.* Ah-<u>kee</u> ess-<u>tah</u> bee-<u>en</u>

348. Let me out here, please. (for.) *Déjeme aquí, por favor.*
 <u>Deh</u>-heh-meh ah-<u>kee</u>, por fah-<u>vor</u>

349. Can you wait for me here? (for.) *¿Me puede esperar aquí?*
 Meh <u>pweh</u>-deh ess-peh-<u>rar</u> ah-<u>kee</u>

350. Wait for me here, please (for.) *Espéreme aquí, por favor.*
 Ess-<u>peh</u>-reh-meh ah-<u>kee</u>, por fah-<u>vor</u>

351. Can you take me back? (for.) *¿Me puede llevar de regreso?*
 Meh <u>pweh</u>-deh yeh-<u>var</u> deh reh-<u>greh</u>-soh

352. Keep the change. (for.) *Quédese con el cambio.*
 <u>Keh</u>-deh-seh kohn el <u>kahm</u>-bee-oh

353. Where is the bus stop?   *¿Dónde está la parada del autobús?*
Dohn-deh ess-**tah** lah pah-**rah**-dah del ow-toh-**boos**

354. Does the bus to . . . stop here?   *¿Para aquí el autobús a . . . ?*
Pah-rah ah-**kee** el ow-toh-**boos** ah

355. At what time does the bus to . . . go by?
¿A qué hora pasa el autobús a . . . ?
Ah keh **oh**-rah **pah**-sah el ow-toh-**boos** ah

356. What's the fare?   *¿Cuánto cuesta el pasaje?*
Kwahn-toh **kwess**-tah el pah-**sah**-heh

357. Is it still a long way to . . . ?
¿Falta mucho para llegar a . . . ?
Fahl-tah **moo**-choh **pah**-rah yeh-**gar** ah

358. Do you go as far as . . . ? (for.)   *¿Llega hasta . . . ?*
Yeh-gah **ahss**-tah

359. Do you go by . . . ? (for.)   *¿Pasa por . . . ?*   **Pah**-sah por

360. Please let me know where to get off. (for.)
Por favor avíseme dónde bajarme.
Por fah-**vor** ah-**vee**-seh-meh **dohn**-deh bah-**har**-meh

361. What's the nearest subway station?
¿Cuál es la estación de metro más cercana?
Kwahl ess lah ess-tah-see-**ohn** deh **meh**-troh mahss
sehr-**kah**-nah

362. Where can I buy a ticket?
¿Dónde puedo comprar un boleto?
Dohn-deh **pweh**-doh kohm-**prar** oon boh-**leh**-toh

363. One ticket, please.   *Un boleto, por favor.*
Oon boh-**leh**-toh por fah-**vor**

364. What's the station for the museum?
¿Cuál es la estación para el museo?
Kwahl ess lah ess-tah-see-**ohn** **pah**-rah el moo-**seh**-oh

365. (Where) Must I transfer to get to . . . ?
¿(Dónde) Debo transbordar para llegar a . . . ?
(**Dohn**-deh) **Deh**-boh trahns-bor-**dar** **pah**-rah yeh-**gar** ah

366. Where can I rent a car?
    ¿Dónde puedo alquilar/ rentar un auto?
    <u>Dohn</u>-deh <u>pweh</u>-doh ahl-kee-<u>lar</u>/ren-<u>tar</u> oon <u>ow</u>-toh

367. I would like to rent a car (with air conditioning).
    Quisiera alquilar/rentar un auto (con aire acondicionado).
    Kee-see-<u>eh</u>-rah ahl-kee-<u>lar</u>/ren-<u>tar</u> oon <u>ow</u>-toh (kohn <u>I</u>-reh
    ah-kohn-dee-see-oh-<u>nah</u>-doh)

368. How much is the rate per hour/day/week?
    ¿Cuánto cuesta el alquiler por hora/día/semana?
    <u>Kwahn</u>-toh <u>kwess</u>-tah el ahl-kee-<u>lehr</u> por <u>oh</u>-rah/<u>dee</u>-ah/
    seh-<u>mah</u>-nah

369. Does it include insurance?   *¿Incluye seguro?*
    Een-<u>kloo</u>-yeh seh-<u>goo</u>-roh

370. Do you have a highway/city map? (for.)
    ¿Tiene un mapa de carreteras/de la ciudad?
    Tee-<u>eh</u>-neh oon <u>mah</u>-pah deh kah-reh-<u>teh</u>-rahss/deh lah
    <u>see</u>-oo-dahd

371. What's the speed limit?   *¿Cuál es el límite de velocidad?*
    Kwahl ess el <u>lee</u>-mee-teh deh vel-oh-see-<u>dahd</u>

372. Do you know where there's a parking lot? (for.)
    ¿Sabe dónde hay un estacionamiento?
    <u>Sah</u>-beh <u>dohn</u>-deh I oon ess-tah-see-oh-nah-mee-<u>en</u>-toh

373. What's the rate?   *¿Cuál es la tarifa?*
    Kwahl ess lah tah-<u>ree</u>-fah

374. Do you charge by the hour/fraction of an hour?
    ¿Cobran por hora/por fracción?
    <u>Koh</u>-brahn por <u>oh</u>-rah/por frahk-see-<u>ohn</u>

375. Can I park here?   *¿Puedo estacionarme aquí?*
    <u>Pweh</u>-doh ess-tah-see-oh-<u>nar</u>-meh ah-<u>kee</u>

376. For how long?   *¿Por cuánto tiempo?*
    Por <u>kwahn</u>-toh tee-<u>em</u>-poh

377. Do I need to put coins in the parking meter?
    ¿Necesito poner monedas en el parquímetro?
    Neh-seh-<u>see</u>-toh poh-<u>nehr</u> moh-<u>neh</u>-dahss en el
    par-<u>kee</u>-meh-troh

378. I don't want to get a ticket.
No quiero que me pongan una multa.
Noh kee-<u>eh</u>-roh keh meh <u>pohn</u>-gahn <u>oo</u>-nah <u>mool</u>-tah

379. Where is there a gas station around here?
¿Dónde hay una gasolinera por aquí?
<u>Dohn</u>-deh I <u>oo</u>-nah gah-soh-lee-<u>neh</u>-rah por ah-<u>kee</u>

380. Fill it up, please.   *Lleno, por favor.*   <u>Yeh</u>-noh, por fah-<u>vor</u>

381. Can you check the oil? (for.)   *¿Puede checar el aceite?*
<u>Pweh</u>-deh cheh-<u>kar</u> el ah-<u>say</u>-teh

   . . . the tire pressure?   . . . *la presión?*   lah preh-see-<u>ohn</u>

A PLACE TO STAY

382. I want to stay in a (cheap/fancy) hotel.
Quiero hospedarme en un hotel (barato/de lujo).
Kee-<u>eh</u>-roh ohss-peh-<u>dar</u>-meh en oon oh-<u>tel</u> (bah-<u>rah</u>-toh/deh <u>loo</u>-hoh)

   . . . a hotel near the downtown area.
   . . . *un hotel cerca del centro.*
   oon oh-<u>tel</u> <u>sehr</u>-kah del <u>sen</u>-troh

   . . . a bed-and-breakfast.   . . . *una pensión con desayuno.*
   <u>oo</u>-nah pen-see-<u>ohn</u> kohn deh-sah-<u>yoo</u>-noh

383. I am looking for a (youth) hostel.
Estoy buscando un albergue (juvenil).
Ess-<u>toy</u> boos-<u>kahn</u>-doh oon ahl-<u>behr</u>-geh (hoo-veh-<u>neel</u>)

   . . . a guesthouse.   . . . *una casa de huéspedes.*
   <u>oo</u>-nah <u>kah</u>-sah deh <u>wess</u>-peh-dess

   . . . a place to sleep.   . . . *un lugar donde dormir.*
   oon loo-<u>gar</u> <u>dohn</u>-deh dor-<u>meer</u>

   . . . a place to camp.   . . . *un lugar donde acampar.*
   oon loo-<u>gar</u> <u>dohn</u>-deh ah-kahm-<u>par</u>

384. How much is a room per night?
¿Cuánto cuesta la habitación por noche?
<u>Kwahn</u>-toh <u>kwess</u>-tah lah ah-bee-tah-see-<u>ohn</u> por <u>noh</u>-cheh

   . . . per week?   . . . *por semana?*   por seh-<u>mah</u>-nah

   . . . per person?   . . . *por persona?*   por pehr-<u>soh</u>-nah

385. Does it include meals?   ¿Incluye comidas?
     Een-<u>kloo</u>-yeh koh-<u>mee</u>-dahss

     . . . breakfast?   . . . el desayuno?   el deh-sah yoo-noh

     . . . dinner?   . . . la cena?   lah <u>seh</u>-nah

386. I have a reservation.   Tengo una reservación.
     <u>Ten</u>-goh <u>oo</u>-nah reh-sehr-vah-see-<u>ohn</u>

387. My name is . . .   Mi nombre es . . .
     Mee <u>nohm</u>-breh ess . . .

388. Can I make a reservation (for today)?
     ¿Puedo hacer una reservación (para hoy)?
     <u>Pweh</u>-doh ah-<u>sehr</u> <u>oo</u>-nah reh-sehr-vah-see-<u>ohn</u> (<u>pah</u>-rah oy)

389. I want to make a reservation for tomorrow.
     Quiero hacer una reservación para mañana.
     Kee-<u>eh</u>-roh ah-<u>ser</u> <u>oo</u>-nah reh-sehr-vah-see-<u>ohn</u> <u>pah</u>-rah
     mah-<u>nyah</u>-nah

     . . . for next week.   . . . para la semana próxima.
     <u>pah</u>-rah lah seh-<u>mah</u>-nah <u>prohk</u>-see-mah

390. Do you have rooms available? (for.)
     ¿Tiene habitaciones disponibles?
     Tee-<u>eh</u>-neh ah-bee-tah-see-<u>oh</u>-ness dees-poh-<u>nee</u>-bless

391. I would like a single/double room.
     Quisiera una habitación sencilla/doble.
     Kee-see-<u>eh</u>-rah <u>oo</u>-nah ah-bee-tah-see-<u>ohn</u> sen-<u>see</u>-yah/<u>doh</u>-bleh

     . . . a room with a bathroom/bathtub.
     . . . una habitación con baño/tina.
     <u>oo</u>-nah ah-bee-tah-see-<u>ohn</u> kohn <u>bah</u>-nyoh/<u>tee</u>-nah

392. I want a room with air conditioning.
     Quiero una habitación con aire acondicionado.
     Kee-<u>eh</u>-roh <u>oo</u>-nah ah-bee-tah-see-<u>ohn</u> kohn <u>I</u>-reh
     ah-kohn-dee-see-oh-<u>nah</u>-doh

393. Do you have a room with a view? (for.)
     ¿Tiene una habitación con vista?
     Tee-<u>eh</u>-neh <u>oo</u>-nah ah-bee-tah-see-<u>ohn</u> kohn <u>vees</u>-tah

... a (non) smoking room?
... una habitación de (no) fumar?
oo-nah ah-bee-tah-see-<u>ohn</u> deh (noh) foo-<u>mar</u>

... two (neighboring) rooms?
... dos habitaciones lado a lado?
dohss ah-bee-tah-see-<u>oh</u>-ness <u>lah</u>-doh ah <u>lah</u>-doh

... a luxury suite?   *... una suite de lujo?*
oo-nah sweet de <u>loo</u>-hoh

394. May I see the room?   *¿Puedo ver la habitación?*
<u>Pweh</u>-doh vehr lah ah-bee-tah-see-<u>ohn</u>

395. Does it have hot water?   *¿Tiene agua caliente?*
Tee-<u>eh</u>-neh <u>ah</u>-wah kah-lee-<u>en</u>-teh

... cable TV?   *... televisión con cable?*
teh-leh-vee-see-<u>ohn</u> kohn <u>kah</u>-bleh

... Internet access?   *... conexión a la red?*
koh-nek-see-<u>ohn</u> ah lah red

... Wi-Fi?   *... conexión inalámbrica?*
koh-nek-see-<u>ohn</u> een-ah-<u>lahm</u>-bree-kah

... kitchenette?   *... cocineta?*   **koh-see-<u>neh</u>-tah**

396. Is there laundry service?   *¿Hay servicio de lavandería?*
I sehr-<u>vee</u>-see-oh de lah-vahn-deh-<u>ree</u>-ah

... parking?   *... estacionamiento?*
ess-tah-see-oh-nah-mee-<u>en</u>-toh

397. I will be staying for one night/two nights.
Me voy a quedar una noche/dos noches.
Meh voy ah keh-<u>dar</u> oo-nah <u>noh</u>-cheh/dohss <u>noh</u>-chess

... one week/two weeks.   *... una semana/dos semanas.*
oo-nah seh-<u>mah</u>-nah/dohss seh-<u>mah</u>-nahss

398. I don't know how long I will be staying.
No sé por cuánto tiempo me voy a quedar.
Noh seh por <u>kwahn</u>-toh tee-<u>em</u>-poh meh voy ah keh-<u>dar</u>

399. I want to stay another night.
Quiero quedarme una noche más.
Kee-<u>eh</u>-roh keh-<u>dar</u>-meh oo-nah <u>noh</u>-cheh mahss

400.   Can I pay in advance?   *¿Puedo pagar por adelantado?*
       <u>Pweh</u>-doh pah-<u>gar</u> por ah-del-ahn-<u>tah</u>-doh

401.   Do you take credit cards?   *¿Aceptan tarjetas de crédito?*
       Ah-<u>sep</u>-tahn tar-<u>heh</u>-tahs deh <u>kreh</u>-dee-toh

       . . . cash?   . . . *efectivo?*   eh-fek-<u>tee</u>-voh

402.   Is there a strong box in the room?
       ¿Hay una caja de seguridad en la habitación?
       I <u>oo</u>-nah <u>kah</u>-hah deh seh-<u>goo</u>-ree-dahd en lah
       ah-bee-tah-see-<u>ohn</u>

403.   Should I leave my valuables at the desk?
       ¿Debo dejar mis objetos de valor en la recepción?
       <u>Deh</u>-boh deh-<u>hahr</u> mees ohb-<u>heh</u>-tohss deh vah-<u>lor</u> en lah
       reh-sep-see-<u>ohn</u>

404.   Can somebody help me with my luggage?
       ¿Me puede ayudar alguien con mis maletas?
       Meh <u>pweh</u>-deh ah-yoo-<u>dar</u> <u>ahl</u>-gee-en kohn mees
       mah-<u>leh</u>-tahss

405.   By what time do I need to check out?
       ¿A qué hora debo dejar libre la habitación?
       Ah keh <u>oh</u>-rah <u>deh</u>-boh deh-<u>har</u> <u>lee</u>-breh lah
       ah-bee-tah-see-<u>ohn</u>

406.   At what time do you serve breakfast/dinner?
       ¿A qué hora sirven el desayuno/la cena?
       Ah keh <u>oh</u>-rah <u>seer</u>-ven el deh-sah-<u>yoo</u>-noh/lah <u>seh</u>-nah

407.   Until what time do you serve breakfast/dinner?
       ¿Hasta qué hora sirven el desayuno/la cena?
       <u>Ahss</u>-tah keh <u>oh</u>-rah <u>seer</u>-ven el deh-sah-<u>yoo</u>-noh/lah <u>seh</u>-nah

408.   Can you wake me up at . . . ?
       ¿Me puede despertar a las . . . ?
       Meh <u>pweh</u>-deh dess-pehr-<u>tar</u> ah lahss

409.   Where is the elevator?   *¿Dónde está el ascensor/elevador?*
       <u>Dohn</u>-deh ess-<u>tah</u> el ah-sen-<u>sor</u>/el-eh-vah-<u>dor</u>

       . . . the dining room?   . . . *el comedor?*   el koh-meh-<u>dor</u>

410. Is there a workout room? ¿*Hay un cuarto de ejercicios?*
I oon **kwar**-toh deh eh-hehr-**see**-see-ohss

. . . a swimming pool? . . . *una piscina/alberca?*
oo-nah pee-**see**-nah/ahl-**behr**-kah

. . . a business center? . . . *un centro de negocios?*
oon **sen**-troh deh neh-**goh**-see-ohss

411. Can you clean the room now/later? (for.)
¿*Puede asear la habitación ahora/más tarde?*
Pweh-deh ah-seh-**ar** lah ah-bee-tah-see-**ohn** ah-**oh**-rah/
mahss **tar**-deh

412. These sheets are dirty. *Estas sábanas están sucias.*
Ess-tahss **sah**-bah-nahss ess-**tahn** **soo**-see-ahss

413. I need clean sheets. *Necesito sábanas limpias.*
Neh-seh-**see**-toh **sah**-bah-nahss **leem**-pee-ahss

. . . clean towels. . . . *toallas limpias.*
twah-yahss **leem**-pee-ahss

. . . another blanket. . . . *otra cobija/manta.*
oh-trah koh-**bee**-hah/**mahn**-tah

414. Can you bring me another pillow? (for.)
¿*Me puede traer otra almohada/cojín?*
Meh **pweh**-deh trah-**ehr** **oh**-trah ahl-moh-**ah**-dah/koh-**heen**

. . . an extra bed? . . . *una cama extra?*
oo-nah **kah**-mah **ek**-strah

415. How does the heat work? ¿*Cómo funciona la calefacción?*
Koh-moh foon-see-**oh**-nah lah kah-leh-fahk-see-**ohn**

. . . the air conditioning work? . . . *el aire acondicionado?*
el **I**-reh ah-kohn-dee-see-oh-**nah**-doh

416. I lost my key. *Perdí mi llave.* Pehr-**dee** mee **yah**-veh

417. My room number is . . . *Mi número de cuarto es . . .*
Mee **noo**-meh-roh deh **kwar**-toh ess

418. I'm leaving. *Ya me voy.* Yah meh voy

419. The bill, please. *La cuenta, por favor.*
Lah **kwen**-tah, por fah-**vor**

420.   I think there is a mistake in the bill.
       Creo que hay un error en la cuenta.
       <u>Kreh</u>-oh keh I oon eh-<u>ror</u> en lah <u>kwen</u>-tah

421.   I didn't make these calls.   *Yo no hice estas llamadas.*
       Yoh noh <u>ee</u>-seh <u>ess</u>-tahss yah-<u>mah</u>-dahss

422.   I didn't take anything from the minibar.
       No tomé nada del minibar.
       Noh toh-<u>meh</u> <u>nah</u>-dah del mee-nee-bar

423.   Can I leave my luggage here for a while?
       ¿Puedo dejar mi equipaje aquí por un rato?
       <u>Pweh</u>-doh deh-<u>hahr</u> mee eh-kee-<u>pah</u>-heh ah-<u>kee</u> por oon <u>rah</u>-toh

424.   I want to rent an apartment.
       Quiero rentar/alquilar un apartamento.
       Kee-<u>eh</u>-roh ren-<u>tar</u>/ahl-kee-<u>lar</u> oon ah-par-tah-<u>men</u>-toh

       . . . an (a furnished) apartment.
       . . . *un piso (amueblado). (Sp.)*   oon <u>pee</u>-soh (ah-mweh-<u>blah</u>-doh)

       . . . a cabin.   . . . *una cabaña.*   <u>oo</u>-nah kah-<u>bah</u>-nyah

       . . . a house.   . . . *una casa.*   <u>oo</u>-nah <u>kah</u>-sah

425.   How many rooms/bathrooms does it have?
       ¿Cuántos cuartos/baños tiene?
       <u>Kwahn</u>-tohss <u>kwar</u>-tohss/<u>bah</u>-nyohss tee-<u>eh</u>-neh

426.   Do I need to give a deposit?   *¿Necesito dar un depósito?*
       Neh-seh-<u>see</u>-toh dar oon deh-<u>poh</u>-see-toh

EATING & DRINKING

427.   I'm (not) (very) hungry.   *(No) Tengo (mucha) hambre.*
       (Noh) <u>Ten</u>-goh (<u>moo</u>-chah) <u>ahm</u>-breh

       . . . thirsty.   . . . *sed.*   sehd

428.   I'm really really hungry. [lit. I'm dying from hunger]
       Me muero de hambre.   Meh <u>mweh</u>-roh deh <u>ahm</u>-breh

       . . . thirsty.   . . . *de sed.*   deh sehd

429.   I want to eat/drink (something).   *Quiero comer/beber (algo).*
       Kee-<u>eh</u>-roh koh-<u>mehr</u>/beh-<u>behr</u> (<u>ahl</u>-goh)

430.   I don't want to eat/drink (anything).
       No quiero comer/beber (nada).
       Noh kee-<u>eh</u>-roh koh-<u>mehr</u>/beh-<u>behr</u> (<u>nah</u>-dah)

431.   Where do you all want to eat?   *¿Dónde quieren comer?*
       <u>Dohn</u>-deh kee-<u>eh</u>-ren koh-<u>mehr</u>

432.   When can we eat?   *¿Cúando podemos comer?*
       <u>Kwahn</u>-doh poh-<u>deh</u>-mohss koh-<u>mehr</u>

433.   It's time for breakfast.   *Es hora de desayunar.*
       Ess <u>oh</u>-rah deh deh-sah-yoo-<u>nar</u>

       . . . for an early lunch.   . . . *de almorzar.*   deh ahl-mor-<u>sar</u>
       . . . for lunch.   . . . *de comer.*   deh koh-<u>mehr</u>

434.   I feel like eating an early dinner.   *Tengo ganas de merendar.*
       <u>Ten</u>-goh <u>gah</u>-nahss deh meh-ren-<u>dar</u>

       . . . dinner.   . . . *de cenar.*   deh seh-<u>nar</u>
       . . . a snack.   . . . *de un tentempié.*
       deh oon ten-tem-pee-<u>eh</u>

435.   Can you recommend a (good) restaurant? (for.)
       ¿Me puede recomendar un (buen) restaurante?
       Meh <u>pweh</u>-deh reh-koh-men-<u>dar</u> oon bwen ress-tow-<u>rahn</u>-teh

       . . . a (good) snack bar?   . . . *una (buena) cafetería?*
       <u>oo</u>-nah (<u>bweh</u>-nah) kah-feh-teh-<u>ree</u>-ah

       . . . a (good) coffee shop?   . . . *un (buen) café?*
       oon (bwen) kah-<u>feh</u>

       . . . a (good) bar?   . . . *un (buen) bar?*   oon (bwen) bar

436.   I would like to try the local food.
       Me gustaría probar la comida típica.
       Meh goos-tah-<u>ree</u>-ah proh-<u>bar</u> lah koh-<u>mee</u>-dah <u>tee</u>-pee-kah

437.   I want to go to a fast food restaurant.
       Quiero ir a un restaurante de comida rápida.
       Kee-<u>eh</u>-roh eer ah oon ress-tow-<u>rahn</u>-teh deh koh-<u>mee</u>-dah
       <u>rah</u>-pee-dah

438.   I am looking for a cheap/expensive restaurant.
       Estoy buscando un restaurante barato/caro.
       Ess-<u>toy</u> boos-<u>kahn</u>-doh oon ress-tow-<u>rahn</u>-teh bah-<u>rah</u>-toh/
       <u>kah</u>-roh

439.   Do you know any vegetarian restaurants? (inf.)
       ¿Conoces algún restaurante vegetariano?
       Koh-<u>noh</u>-sess ahl-<u>goon</u> ress-tow <u>rahn</u>-teh
       veh-heh-tah-ree-<u>ah</u>-noh

440.   Let's go to a romantic restaurant.
       Vamos a un restaurante romántico.
       <u>Vah</u>-mohss ah oon ress-tow-<u>rahn</u>-teh roh-<u>mahn</u>-tee-koh

       . . . a restaurant with outdoor dining.
       . . . *un restaurante con mesas afuera.*
       oon ress-tow-<u>rahn</u>-teh kohn <u>mehss</u>-ahss ah-<u>fweh</u>-rah

441.   What's the city's best restaurant?
       ¿Cuál es el mejor restaurante de la ciudad?
       Kwahl ess el meh-<u>hor</u> ress-tow-<u>rahn</u>-teh deh la <u>see</u>-oo-dahd

442.   Do you need a reservation?   *¿Se necesita una reservación?*
       Seh neh-seh-<u>see</u>-tah <u>oo</u>-nah reh-sehr-vah-see-<u>ohn</u>

443.   Will I need to wear a jacket?
       ¿Tendré que usar chaqueta/saco? (L. Am.)
       Ten-<u>dreh</u> keh oo-<u>sar</u> chah-<u>keh</u>-tah/<u>sah</u>-koh

444.   I want to make a reservation for lunch/dinner.
       Quiero hacer una reservación para comer/cenar.
       Kee-<u>eh</u>-roh ah-<u>sehr</u> <u>oo</u>-nah reh-sehr-vah-see-<u>ohn</u> <u>pah</u>-rah
       koh-<u>mehr</u>/seh-<u>nar</u>

       . . . for (the day after) tomorrow.
       . . . *para (pasado) mañana.*
       <u>pah</u>-rah (pah-<u>sah</u>-doh) mah-<u>nyah</u>-nah

       . . . for two-thirty p.m.
       . . . *para las dos y media de la tarde.*
       <u>pah</u>-rah lahss dohss ee <u>meh</u>-dee-ah deh lah <u>tar</u>-deh

       . . . for tonight.   . . . *para esta noche.*
       <u>pah</u>-rah <u>ess</u>-tah <u>noh</u>-cheh

445.   Do you have a table for tomorrow night? (for.)
       ¿Tiene una mesa para mañana en la noche?
       Tee-<u>eh</u>-neh <u>oo</u>-nah <u>meh</u>-sah <u>pah</u>-rah mah-<u>nyah</u>-nah en lah
       <u>noh</u>-cheh

       . . . for eight p.m.?   . . . *para las ocho de la noche?*
       <u>pah</u>-rah lahss <u>oh</u>-choh deh lah <u>noh</u>-cheh

. . . for two people?   . . . *para dos personas?*
<u>pah</u>-rah dohss pehr-<u>soh</u>-nahss

446. Let's go have [something before/after eating].
Vamos a tomar algo antes/después de comer.
<u>Vah</u>-mohss ah toh-<u>mar</u> <u>ahl</u>-goh <u>ahn</u>-tehss/dess-<u>pwess</u> deh
koh-<u>mehr</u>

. . . a drink.   . . . *un trago.*   oon <u>trah</u>-goh

. . . a beer.   . . . *una cerveza.*   <u>oo</u>-nah sehr-<u>veh</u>-sah

. . . a glass of wine.   . . . *una copa de vino.*
<u>oo</u>-nah <u>koh</u>-pah deh <u>vee</u>-noh

. . . red wine mixed with fruit and lemonade.
. . . *una sangría. (Sp.)*   <u>oo</u>-nah sahn-<u>gree</u>-ah

. . . a drink before lunch.   . . . *un aperitivo.*
oon ah-peh-ree-<u>tee</u>-voh

. . . some coffee.   . . . *un café.*   oon kah-<u>feh</u>

447. I want to try some traditional Spanish hors d'oeuvres.
Quiero probar unas tapas.
Kee-<u>eh</u>-roh proh-<u>bar</u> <u>oo</u>-nahss <u>tah</u>-pahss

448. We need a table for four (people).
Necesitamos una mesa para cuatro (personas).
Neh-seh-see-<u>tah</u>-mohss <u>oo</u>-nah <u>meh</u>-sah <u>pah</u>-rah <u>kwah</u>-troh
(per-<u>soh</u>-nahss)

. . . a table in the (non) smoking section.
. . . *una mesa en la sección de (no) fumar.*
<u>oo</u>-nah <u>meh</u>-sah en lah sek-see-<u>ohn</u> deh (noh) foo-<u>mar</u>

449. We want a table outside/inside.
Queremos una mesa afuera/adentro.
Keh-<u>reh</u>-mohss <u>oo</u>-nah <u>meh</u>-sah ah-<u>fweh</u>-rah/ah-<u>den</u>-troh

. . . by the window.   . . . *cerca de la ventana.*
<u>sehr</u>-cah deh lah ven-<u>tah</u>-nah

. . . far from the kitchen.   . . . *lejos de la cocina.*
<u>leh</u>-hohss deh lah koh-<u>see</u>-nah

450. Can we sit here?   *¿Nos podemos sentar aquí?*
Nohss poh-<u>deh</u>-mohss sen-<u>tar</u> ah-<u>kee</u>

451. I made a reservation.   *Hice una reservación.*
<u>Ee</u>-seh <u>oo</u>-nah reh-sehr-vah-see-<u>ohn</u>

452. My name is . . .   *Mi nombre es . . .*   Mee <u>nohm</u>-breh ess . . .

453. Should I call the waiter/waitress?
      ¿Llamo al camarero/mesera?
      <u>Yah</u>-moh ahl kah-mah-<u>reh</u>-roh/meh-<u>seh</u>-rah

454. Waiter! (lit. young man)   *¡Joven!*   <u>Hoh</u>-ven
      Waiter!   *¡Camarero!*   Kah-mah-<u>reh</u>-roh

455. Miss!   *¡Señorita!*   Seh-nyoh-<u>ree</u>-tah

456. Can you bring us the menu?
      ¿Nos puede traer la carta/el menú?
      Nohss <u>pweh</u>-deh trah-<u>ehr</u> lah <u>kar</u>-tah/el meh-<u>noo</u>

      . . . the wine list?   . . . *la carta de vinos?*
      lah <u>kar</u>-tah deh <u>vee</u>-nohss

      . . . a children's menu?   . . . *una carta/un menú para niños?*
      <u>oo</u>-nah <u>kar</u>-tah/oon meh-<u>noo</u> <u>pah</u>-rah <u>nee</u>-nyohss

457. Do you have a menu in English? (for.)
      ¿Tiene una carta/un menú en inglés?
      Tee-<u>eh</u>-neh <u>oo</u>-nah <u>kar</u>-tah/oon meh-<u>noo</u> en een-<u>gless</u>

458. We are ready to order.   *Estamos listos para ordenar.*
      Ess-<u>tah</u>-mohss <u>lees</u>-tohss <u>pah</u>-rah or-deh-nar

459. What do you recommend?   *¿Qué nos recomienda?*
      Keh nohss reh-koh-mee-<u>en</u>-dah

460. What's the house specialty?
      ¿Cuál es la especialidad de la casa?
      Kwahl ess lah ess-peh-see-ahl-ee-<u>dahd</u> deh lah <u>kah</u>-sah

461. Do you have vegetarian dishes?
      ¿Tiene platillos vegetarianos?
      Tee-<u>eh</u>-neh plah-<u>tee</u>-yohss veh-heh-tah-ree-<u>ah</u>-nohss

      . . . low-calorie dishes?   . . . *bajos en calorías?*
      <u>bah</u>-hohss en kah-loh-<u>ree</u>-ahss

462. I need a (clean) napkin.   *Necesito una servilleta (limpia).*
      Neh-seh-<u>see</u>-toh <u>oo</u>-nah sehr-vee-<u>yeh</u>-tah (<u>leem</u>-pee-ah)

      . . . (clean) silverware.   . . . *unos cubiertos (limpios).*
      <u>oo</u>-nohss koo-bee-<u>ehr</u>-tohss (<u>leem</u>-pee-ohss)

. . . a spoon.   . . . *una cuchara.*   <u>oo</u>-nah koo-<u>chah</u>-rah

. . . a fork.   . . . *un tenedor.*   oon ten-eh-<u>dor</u>

. . . a knife.   . . . *un cuchillo.*   oon koo-<u>chee</u>-yoh

. . . a teaspoon.   . . . *una cucharita.*
<u>oo</u>-nah koo-chah-<u>ree</u>-tah

463. Can you bring us an extra plate?
¿Nos puede traer otro plato?
<u>Nohss</u> <u>pweh</u>-deh trah-<u>ehr</u> <u>oh</u>-troh <u>plah</u>-toh

. . . more bread?   . . . *más pan?*   mahss pahn

464. What do you want to eat for breakfast? (inf.)
¿Qué quieres desayunar?
Keh kee-<u>eh</u>-ress deh-sah-yoo-<u>nar</u>

465. For breakfast I would like cereal with milk.
Para desayunar me gustaría cereal con leche.
<u>Pah</u>-rah deh-sah-yoo-<u>nar</u> meh goos-tah-<u>ree</u>-ah seh-reh-<u>ahl</u>
kohn <u>leh</u>-cheh

. . . oatmeal.   . . . *avena.*   ah-<u>veh</u>-nah

. . . toast (with butter and jam).
. . . *pan tostado (con mantequilla y mermelada).*
pahn tohss-<u>tah</u>-doh (kohn mahn-teh-<u>kee</u>-yah ee
mehr-meh-<u>lah</u>-dah)

. . . toast.   . . . *una tostada. (Sp.)*   <u>oo</u>-nah tohss-<u>tah</u>-dah

. . . pastries.   . . . *pan dulce.*   pahn <u>dool</u>-seh

. . . French toast.   . . . *pan francés.*   pahn frahn-<u>sess</u>

. . . pancakes.   . . . *panqueques. (L. Am.)*   pahn-<u>keh</u>-kess

466. I want scrambled eggs (with ham/bacon).
Quiero huevos revueltos (con jamón/tocino).
Kee-<u>eh</u>-roh <u>weh</u>-vohss reh-<u>vwel</u>-tohss (kohn hah-<u>mohn</u>/
toh-<u>see</u>-noh)

. . . fried eggs.   . . . *huevos fritos.*   <u>weh</u>-vohss <u>free</u>-tohss

. . . poached eggs.   . . . *huevos escalfados.*
<u>weh</u>-vohss ess-kahl-<u>fah</u>-dohss

. . . soft boiled eggs.
. . . *huevos pasados por agua/huevos tibios. (Mex.)*
<u>weh</u>-vohss pah-<u>sah</u>-dohss por <u>ah</u>-wah/<u>weh</u>-vohss <u>tee</u>-bee-ohss

. . . hard-boiled eggs (with mayonnaise).
. . . *huevos duros (con mayonesa).*
<u>weh</u>-vohss <u>doo</u>-rohss (kohn mah-yoh-<u>neh</u>-sah)

. . . a cheese omelette.   . . . *un omelet con queso.*
oon oh-meh-<u>let</u> kohn <u>keh</u>-soh

467. I like my eggs runny.   *Me gustan los huevos no muy cocidos*
Meh <u>goos</u>-tahn lohss <u>weh</u>-vohss noh mooy koh-<u>see</u>-dohss

468. I prefer my eggs dry.   *Yo prefiero los huevos bien cocidos.*
Yoh preh-fee-<u>eh</u>-roh lohss <u>weh</u>-vohss bee-<u>en</u> koh-<u>see</u>-dohss

469. I will have a fresh fruit plate.
Tomaré un plato de fruta fresca.
Toh-mah-<u>reh</u> oon <u>plah</u>-toh deh <u>froo</u>-tah <u>fress</u>-kah

. . . melon   . . . *melón.*   meh-<u>lohn</u>

. . . watermelon.   . . . *sandía.*   sahn-<u>dee</u>-ah

. . . pineapple.   . . . *piña.*   <u>pee</u>-nyah

. . . grapefruit.   . . . *toronja/pomelo. (Sp.)*
toh-<u>rohn</u>-hah/poh-<u>meh</u>-loh

470. To drink, I would like coffee (decaf).   *De tomar me gustaría*
un café (descafeinado).   Deh toh-<u>mar</u> meh goos-tah-<u>ree</u>-ah
un kah-<u>feh</u> (dess-kah-fay-<u>nah</u>-doh)

. . . coffee with milk.   . . . *café con leche.*
kah-<u>feh</u> kohn <u>leh</u>-cheh

. . . (black/chamomile) tea.   . . . *té (negro/de manzanilla).*
teh (<u>neh</u>-groh/deh mahn-sah-<u>nee</u>-yah)

. . . hot/cold chocolate.   . . . *chocolate caliente/frío.*
choh-koh-<u>lah</u>-teh kah-lee-<u>en</u>-teh/<u>free</u>-oh

. . . a glass of milk.   . . . *un vaso de leche.*
oon <u>vah</u>-soh deh <u>leh</u>-cheh

. . . orange juice.   . . . *jugo de naranja.*
<u>hoo</u>-goh deh nah-<u>rahn</u>-hah

. . . orange juice.   . . . *zumo de naranja. (Sp.)*
<u>soo</u>-moh deh nah-<u>rahn</u>-hah

471. For lunch, I'm going to order the set menu.
Para comer voy a pedir el menú del día.
<u>Pah</u>-rah koh-<u>mehr</u> voy ah peh-<u>deer</u> el meh-<u>noo</u> del <u>dee</u>-ah

. . . the set menu.   . . . *la comida corrida. (Mex.)*
lah koh-<u>mee</u>-dah koh-<u>ree</u>-dah

. . . à la carte.   . . . *a la carta.* ah lah <u>kar</u>-tah

472. Is the soup good?   *¿Está buena la sopa?*
Ess-<u>tah</u> <u>bweh</u>-nah lah <u>soh</u>-pah

473. As a starter I would like the soup of the day.
Como primer plato quisiera la sopa del día.
<u>Koh</u>-moh pree-<u>mehr</u> <u>plah</u>-toh kee-see-<u>eh</u>-rah lah <u>soh</u>-pah del <u>dee</u>-ah

. . . vegetable soup.   . . . *sopa de verduras/legumbres. (Sp.)*
<u>soh</u>-pah de vehr-<u>doo</u>-rahss/leh-<u>goom</u>-bress

. . . noodle soup.   . . . *sopa de fideos.*
<u>soh</u>-pah deh fee-<u>deh</u>-ohss

. . . lentil soup.   . . . *sopa de lentejas.*
<u>soh</u>-pah deh len-<u>teh</u>-hahss

. . . chicken broth (with rice).
. . . *caldo/consomé de pollo (con arroz).*
<u>kahl</u>-doh/kohn-soh-<u>meh</u> deh <u>poh</u>-yoh (kohn ah-<u>rohss</u>)

. . . rice.   . . . *arroz.* ah-<u>rohss</u>

. . . meat-filled pastry.   . . . *empanadas. (L. Am.)*
em-pah-<u>nah</u>-dahss

. . . cold vegetable soup.   . . . *gazpacho. (Sp.)* gahss-<u>pah</u>-choh

474. This soup is cold.   *Esta sopa está fría.*
<u>Ess</u>-tah <u>soh</u>-pah ess-<u>tah</u> <u>free</u>-ah

475. There's a hair in my soup!   *¡Hay un pelo en mi sopa!*
I oon <u>peh</u>-loh en mee <u>soh</u>-pah

476. Bring me a (green/mixed) salad.
Tráigame una ensalada (verde/mixta).
<u>Tri</u>-gah-meh <u>oo</u>-nah en-sah-<u>lah</u>-dah (<u>vehr</u>-deh/<u>meeks</u>-tah)

. . . a cucumber salad.   . . . *una ensalada de pepino.*
<u>oo</u>-nah en-sah-<u>lah</u>-dah deh peh-<u>pee</u>-noh

. . . a tomato salad.   . . . *una ensalada de tomate.*
<u>oo</u>-nah en-sah-<u>lah</u>-dah deh toh-<u>mah</u>-teh

477. How's the chicken?   *¿Cómo está el pollo?*
<u>Koh</u>-moh ess-<u>tah</u> el <u>poh</u>-yoh

478. As a main dish I would like grilled chicken.
Como plato principal quisiera pollo a la parrilla.
<u>Koh</u>-moh <u>plah</u>-toh preen-see-<u>pahl</u> kee-see-eh-rah <u>poh</u>-yoh ah
lah pah-<u>ree</u>-yah

   . . . fried chicken.   . . . *pollo frito.*   <u>poh</u>-yoh <u>free</u>-toh

   . . . chicken breast.   . . . *pechuga de pollo.*
peh-<u>choo</u>-gah de <u>poh</u>-yoh

   . . . chicken thigh and leg.   . . . *pierna y muslo.*
pee-<u>ehr</u>-nah ee <u>moos</u>-loh

   . . . duck (in blackberry sauce).
   . . . *pato (en salsa de zarzamora).*
<u>pah</u>-toh (en <u>sahl</u>-sah deh sar-sah-<u>moh</u>-rah)

   . . . (stuffed) turkey.   . . . *pavo (relleno).*
<u>pah</u>-voh (reh-<u>yeh</u>-noh)

   . . . roast beef.   . . . *carne asada.*   <u>kar</u>-neh ah-<u>sah</u>-dah

   . . . beef steak.   . . . *bife. (Arg.)*   <u>bee</u>-feh

   . . . steak.   . . . *solomillo. (Sp.)*   soh-loh-<u>mee</u>-yoh

479. I prefer it cooked rare.
Lo prefiero medio rojo/poco hecho. (Sp.)
Loh preh-fee-<u>eh</u>-roh <u>meh</u>-dee-oh <u>roh</u>-hoh/<u>poh</u>-koh <u>eh</u>-choh

   . . . cooked medium.   . . . *término medio/medio hecho. (Sp.)*
<u>tehr</u>-mee-noh <u>meh</u>-dee-oh/<u>meh</u>-dee-oh <u>eh</u>-choh

   . . . cooked well done.   . . . *bien cocido/bien hecho. (Sp.)*
bee-<u>en</u> koh-<u>see</u>-doh/bee-<u>en</u> <u>eh</u>-choh

480. I'll order meatballs.   *Pediré albóndigas.*
Peh-dee-<u>reh</u> ahl-<u>bohn</u>-dee-gahss

   . . . a hamburger.   . . . *una hamburguesa.*
<u>oo</u>-nah ahm-boor-<u>geh</u>-sah

   . . . pork chop.   . . . *chuleta de cerdo.*
choo-<u>leh</u>-tah deh <u>sehr</u>-doh

   . . . pork loin.   . . . *lomo de cerdo.*   <u>loh</u>-moh deh <u>sehr</u>-doh

   . . . veal scallop.   . . . *escalope de ternera.*
ess-kah-<u>loh</u>-peh deh tehr-<u>neh</u>-rah

   . . . rack of lamb.   . . . *costillas de cordero.*
kohss-<u>tee</u>-yahss deh kor-<u>deh</u>-roh

481. Is the fish fresh?   ¿Está fresco el pescado?
      Ess-_tah_ _fress_-koh el pess-_kah_-doh

482. Where does it come from?   ¿De dónde viene?
      Deh _dohn_-deh vee-_eh_-neh

483. I don't want frozen fish.   No quiero pescado congelado.
      Noh kee-_eh_-roh-pess-_kah_-doh kohn-heh-_lah_-doh

484. I think I'll have filet of fish.
      Creo que comeré filete de pescado.
      Kreh-oh keh koh-mehr-_eh_ fee-_leh_-teh deh pes-_kah_-doh

      . . . fresh tuna fish.   . . . atún fresco.   ah-_toon_ _fress_-koh

      . . . cod fish.   . . . bacalao.   bah-kah-_lah_-oh

      . . . sole fish.   . . . lenguado.   len-_gwah_-doh

      . . . grouper fish.   . . . mero.   _meh_-roh

      . . . red snapper.   . . . huachinango.   wah-chee-_nahn_-goh

      . . . sea bass.   . . . robalo.   roh-_bah_-loh

      . . . salmon.   . . . salmón.   sahl-_mohn_

      . . . trout.   . . . trucha.   _troo_-chah

485. I would prefer the seafood dish.
      Preferiría el plato de mariscos.
      Preh-feh-ree-_ree_-ah el _plah_-toh deh mah-_rees_-kohss

      . . . mussels.   . . . mejillones.   meh-hee-_yoh_-ness

      . . . shrimp.   . . . camarones/gambas.
      kah-mah-_roh_-ness/_gahm_-bahss

      . . . prawns.   . . . langostinos.   lahn-gohss-_tee_-nohss

      . . . lobster.   . . . langosta.   lahn-_gohss_-tah

      . . . squids (in ink).   . . . calamares (en su tinta).
      kah-lah-_mah_-ress

      . . . octopus.   . . . pulpo.   _pool_-poh

486. You have to try the saffron rice with chicken and seafood. (inf.)
      Tienes que probar la paella.
      Tee-_eh_-ness keh proh-_bar_ lah pah-_eh_-yah

487. I just want pasta.   Sólo quiero pasta.
      Soh-loh kee-_eh_-roh _pahss_-tah

488. Is it very spicy?   *¿Es muy picante?*
Ess mooy pee-<u>kahn</u>-teh

489. Does it have a lot of fat?   *¿Tiene mucha grasa?*
Tee-<u>eh</u>-neh <u>moo</u>-chah <u>grah</u>-sah

490. No onions, please.   *Sin cebolla, por favor.*
Seen seh-<u>boh</u>-yah por fah-<u>vor</u>

491. Please do not add salt.   *Por favor no le ponga sal.*
Por fah-<u>vor</u> noh leh <u>pohn</u>-gah sahl

492. I'm allergic to nuts.   *Soy alérgico a las nueces.*
Soy ah-<u>lehr</u>-hee-koh ah lahss <u>nweh</u>-sess

. . . to shellfish.   *. . . a los mariscos.*
ah lohss mah-<u>rees</u>-kohss

493. As a side I would like rice.
De acompañamiento/guarnición quisiera arroz.
Deh ah-kohm-pah-nyah-mee-<u>en</u>-toh/war-nee-see-<u>ohn</u>
kee-see-<u>ehr</u>-ah ah-<u>rohss</u>

. . . rice with avocado/with fried banana.
. . . arroz con aguacate/con plátano frito.
ah-<u>ross</u> kohn ah-wah-<u>kah</u>-teh/kohn <u>plah</u>-tah-noh <u>free</u>-toh

. . . zucchini.   *. . . calabacita/calabacín. (Sp.)*
kah-lah-bah-<u>see</u>-tah/kah-lah-bah-<u>seen</u>

. . . asparagus.   *. . . espárragos.*   ess-<u>pah</u>-rah-gohss

. . . spinach.   *. . . espinaca.*   ess-pee-<u>nah</u>-cah

. . . chick peas.   *. . . garbanzos.*   gar-<u>bahn</u>-sohss

494. Is it served with French fries?   *¿Se sirve con papas fritas?*
Seh <u>seer</u>-veh kohn <u>pah</u>-pahss <u>free</u>-tahss

. . . French fries?   *. . . patatas fritas? (Sp.)*
pah-<u>tah</u>-tahss <u>free</u>-tahss

. . . a baked potato?   *. . . una papa/patata al horno?*
<u>oo</u>-nah <u>pah</u>-pah/pah-<u>tah</u>-tah ahl <u>ohr</u>-noh

. . . mashed potatoes?   *. . . puré de papa/patata? (Sp.)*
poo-<u>reh</u> deh <u>pah</u>-pah/pah-<u>tah</u>-tah

495.   Instead, I want vegetables.
       En su lugar, quiero verduras/legumbres. (Sp.)
       En soo loo-gar kee-eh-roh vehr-doo-rahss/leh-goom-bress

       . . . peas.   . . . *chícharos/guisantes. (Sp.)*
       chee-chah-rohss/gee-sahn-tess

       . . . green beans.   . . . *ejotes/judías verdes. (Sp.)*
       eh-hoh-tess/hoo-dee-ahss vehr-dess

       . . . mushrooms.   . . . *hongos/champiñones.*
       ohn-gohss/chahm-pee-nyoh-ness

       . . . carrots.   . . . *zanahorias.*   **sah-nah-oh-ree-ahss**

496.   It's healthier.   *Es más sano.*   **Ess mahss sah-noh**

497.   What do you have to drink?   *¿Qué bebidas tienen?*
       Keh beh-bee-dahss tee-eh-nen

498.   Is the water filtered?   *¿Está filtrada el agua?*
       Ess-tah feel-trah-dah el ah-wah

499.   To drink, I want water.   *De tomar, quiero agua.*
       Deh toh-mar, kee-eh-roh ah-wah

       . . . bottled water.   . . . *agua embotellada.*
       ah-wah em-boh-teh-yah-dah

       . . . mineral water.   . . . *agua mineral.*
       ah-wah mee-neh-rahl

       . . . hibiscus-flower ice tea.   . . . *agua de jamaica.*
       ah-wah deh hah-mi-kah

       . . . a (light/dark) beer.   . . . *una cerveza (clara/oscura).*
       oo-nah sehr-veh-sah (klah-rah/ohss-koo-rah)

       . . . a glass of wine red/white.
       . . . *una copa de vino tinto/blanco.*
       oo-nah koh-pah deh vee-noh teen-toh/blahn-koh

       . . . lemonade/orangeade.   . . . *limonada/naranjada.*
       lee-moh-nah-dah/nah-rahn-hah-dah

       . . . a soft drink.   . . . *un refresco.*   **oon reh-fress-koh**

500.   What soft drinks do you have? (for.)   *¿Qué refrescos tiene?*
       Keh reh-fress-kohss tee-eh-neh

501. Can you bring me a diet soda? (for.)
¿Me puede traer un refresco dietético?
Meh <u>pweh</u>-deh trah-<u>ehr</u> oon roh-<u>fress</u>-koh dee-eh-<u>teh</u>-tee-koh

502. Enjoy!   *¡Buen provecho!*   Bwen proh-<u>veh</u>-choh

503. For dessert, bring me rice pudding. (for.)
De postre, tráigame arroz con leche.
Deh <u>pohss</u>-treh, <u>tri</u>-gah-meh ah-<u>rohss</u> kohn <u>leh</u>-cheh

... peaches in syrup.
... *duraznos/melocotones en almíbar.*
doo-<u>rahss</u>-nohss/meh-loh-koh-<u>toh</u>-ness en ahl-<u>mee</u>-bar

... caramel custard.   ... *flan.*   flahn

... strawberries and cream.   ... *fresas con crema/nata. (Sp.)*
<u>freh</u>-sahss kohn <u>kreh</u>-mah/<u>nah</u>-tah

504. What ice cream flavors do you have?
¿Qué sabores de helado tienen?
Keh sah-<u>boh</u>-ress deh eh-<u>lah</u>-doh tee-<u>eh</u>-nen

505. I would like to order some (vanilla/strawberry/chocolate)
ice cream.
Me gustaría ordenar un helado (de vainilla/fresa/chocolate).
Meh goos-tah-<u>ree</u>-ah or-deh-<u>nar</u> el-<u>ah</u>-doh (deh vi-<u>nee</u>-yah/
<u>freh</u>-sah/cho-koh-<u>lah</u>-teh)

... (lemon/mango/passion fruit) sherbet.
... *nieve (de limón/mango/maracuyá). (Mex.)*
nee-<u>eh</u>-veh (deh lee-<u>mohn</u>/<u>mahn</u>-goh/mah-rah-koo-<u>yah</u>)

... (lemon/raspberry) sherbet.
... *sorbete (de limón/frambuesa). (Sp.)*
sor-<u>beh</u>-teh (deh lee-<u>mohn</u>/frahm-<u>bweh</u>-sah)

... (three-milk) cake.   ... *pastel (de tres leches). (Mex.)*
pahss-<u>tel</u> (deh trehss <u>leh</u>-chess)

... (cheese) cake.   ... *tarta (de queso). (Sp.)*
<u>tar</u>-tah (deh <u>keh</u>-soh)

... (chocolate) cake.
... *torta (de chocolate). (S. Am.)*   <u>tor</u>-tah (deh choh-koh-<u>lah</u>-teh)

506. Let's have dessert somewhere else.
Comamos el postre en otro lado.
Koh-<u>mah</u>-mohss el <u>pohss</u>-treh en <u>oh</u>-troh <u>lah</u>-doh

507. Would you like some coffee? *¿Les gustaría un café?*
Less goos-tah-<u>ree</u>-ah oon kah-<u>feh</u>

   . . . plain coffee.   . . . *café americano.*
kah-<u>feh</u> ah-meh-ree-<u>kah</u>-noh

   . . . coffee with spices and raw sugar.
   . . . *café de olla. (Mex.)*   **kah-<u>feh</u> deh <u>oh</u>-yah**

   . . . espresso (with a dash of milk).
   . . . *expreso (cortado).*   **eks-<u>press</u>-oh (kor-<u>tah</u>-doh)**

508. This needs a little salt/pepper/sugar.
Esto necesita un poco de sal/pimienta/azúcar.
<u>Ess</u>-toh neh-seh-<u>see</u>-tah oon <u>poh</u>-koh deh sahl/pee-mee-<u>en</u>-tah/ah-<u>soo</u>-kar

509. This is delicious/disgusting.   *Esto está delicioso/asqueroso.*
<u>Ess</u>-toh ess-<u>tah</u> deh-lee-see-<u>ohss</u>-oh/ahss-keh-<u>rohss</u>-oh

510. I (don't) want more.   *(No) Quiero más.*
(Noh) Kee-<u>eh</u>-roh mahss

511. Where is the bathroom?
¿Dónde está el baño/los servicios? (Sp.)
<u>Dohn</u>-deh ess-<u>tah</u> el <u>bah</u>-nyoh/lohss sehr-<u>vee</u>-see-ohss

   . . . the men's room?
   . . . *el baño/los servicios para caballeros?*
**el <u>bah</u>-nyoh/lohss sehr-<u>vee</u>-see-ohss <u>pah</u>-rah
kah-bah-<u>yeh</u>-rohss**

   . . . the ladies' room?   . . . *el baño/los servicios para damas?*
el <u>bah</u>-nyoh/lohss sehr-<u>vee</u>-see-ohss <u>pah</u>-rah <u>dah</u>-mahss

512. The check, please.   *La cuenta, por favor.*
Lah <u>kwen</u>-tah por fah-<u>vor</u>

513. Is service/the tip included?
¿Está incluido el servicio/la propina?
Ess-<u>tah</u> een-kloo-<u>ee</u>-doh el sehr-<u>vee</u>-see-oh/lah proh-<u>pee</u>-nah

514. The check is wrong.   *La cuenta está equivocada.*
Lah <u>kwen</u>-tah ess-<u>tah</u> eh-kee-voh-<u>kah</u>-dah

515. We did not order this.   *No pedimos esto.*
Noh peh-<u>dee</u>-mohss <u>ess</u>-toh

516. I want to speak with the manager.
      Quiero hablar con el gerente.
      Kee-<u>eh</u>-roh ah-<u>blar</u> kohn el heh-<u>ren</u>-tch

KEEPING IN TOUCH

517. I need to make a phone call.
      Necesito hacer una llamada telefónica.
      Neh-seh-<u>see</u>-toh ah-<u>sehr</u> <u>oo</u>-nah yah-<u>mah</u>-dah
      teh-leh-<u>foh</u>-nee-kah

      . . . an international call.   . . . *una llamada internacional.*
      <u>oo</u>-nah yah-<u>mah</u>-dah een-tehr-nah-see-oh-<u>nahl</u>

      . . . a collect call.   . . . *una llamada por cobrar.*   <u>oo</u>-nah
      yah-<u>mah</u>-dah por koh-<u>brar</u>

518. Where can I connect to the Internet?
      ¿Dónde puedo conectarme a la red?
      <u>Dohn</u>-deh <u>pweh</u>-doh koh-nek-<u>tar</u>-meh ah lah red

519. I have my own laptop computer.   *Tengo mi propia*
      computadora portátil.   <u>Ten</u>-goh mee <u>proh</u>-pee-ah
      kohm-poo-tah-<u>doh</u>-rah por-<u>tah</u>-teel

      . . . laptop computer.
      . . . *propio ordenador portátil. (Sp.)*
      <u>proh</u>-pree-oh or-deh-nah-<u>dor</u> por-<u>tah</u>-teel

520. Is there (free) Wi-Fi access here?
      ¿Hay acceso inalámbrico (gratis) aquí?
      I ahk-<u>seh</u>-soh een-ahl-<u>ahm</u>-bree-koh (<u>grah</u>-tees) ah-<u>kee</u>

521. I want to send an e-mail.
      Quiero enviar/mandar un correo electrónico.
      Kee-<u>eh</u>-roh en-vee-<u>ar</u>/mahn-<u>dar</u> oon koh-<u>reh</u>-oh
      eh-lek-<u>troh</u>-nee-koh

      . . . a text message.   . . . *un mensaje de texto.*
      oon men-<u>sah</u>-heh deh <u>tex</u>-toh

      . . . a fax.   . . . *un fax.*   oon fax

      . . . a letter (by air mail).   . . . *una carta (por correo aéreo).*
      <u>oo</u>-nah <u>kar</u>-tah (por koh-<u>reh</u>-oh ah-<u>eh</u>-reh-oh)

      . . . a registered letter.   . . . *una carta certificada.*
      <u>oo</u>-nah <u>kar</u>-tah sehr-tee-fee-<u>kah</u>-dah

. . . an express letter.   . . . *una carta urgente.*
oo-nah <u>kar</u>-tah oor-<u>hen</u>-teh

. . . a postcard.   . . . *una postal.*   **oo**-nah pohss-<u>tahl</u>

. . . a package (overnight).
. . . *un paquete (para el día siguiente).*
oon pah-<u>keh</u>-teh (<u>pah</u>-rah el <u>dee</u>-ah see-gee-<u>en</u>-teh)

522. Careful! It's fragile.   *¡Cuidado! Es frágil.*
Kwee-<u>dah</u>-doh ess <u>frah</u>-heel

523. Where is the post office?   *¿Dónde está la oficina de correos?*
<u>Dohn</u>-deh ess-<u>tah</u> lah oh-fee-<u>see</u>-nah deh koh-<u>reh</u>-ohss

. . . the mail box?   . . . *el buzón?*   el boo-<u>sohn</u>

524. Where can I find pen and ink?
¿Dónde puedo encontrar papel y pluma.
<u>Dohn</u>-deh <u>pweh</u>-doh en-kohn-<u>trar</u> pah-<u>pel</u> ee <u>ploo</u>-mah

. . . envelopes?   . . . *sobres?*   <u>soh</u>-bress

. . . postage stamps?   . . . *estampillas/sellos postales?*
ess-tahm-<u>pee</u>-yahss/<u>seh</u>-yohss pohss-<u>tah</u>-less

525. I would like to buy a calling card.
Quisiera comprar una tarjeta telefónica.
Kee-see-<u>eh</u>-rah kohm-<u>prar</u> **oo**-nah tar-<u>heh</u>-tah
teh-leh-<u>foh</u>-nee-kah

. . . a pre-paid cell phone.
. . . *un teléfono celular/móvil pre-pagado.*
oon teh-<u>leh</u>-foh-noh seh-loo-<u>lar</u>/<u>moh</u>-veel preh-pah-<u>gah</u>-doh

. . . a SIM card.   . . . *una tarjeta SIM.*
oo-nah tar-<u>heh</u>-tah seem

526. There's no signal.   *No hay señal.*   Noh I seh-<u>nyahl</u>

527. We must be outside the service area.
Debemos estar fuera del área de servicio.
Deh-<u>beh</u>-mohss ess-<u>tahr</u> <u>fweh</u>-rah del <u>ah</u>-reh-ah deh
sehr-<u>vee</u>-see-oh

528. What's your e-mail address?
¿Cuál es tu dirección de correo electrónico?
Kwahl ess too dee-rek-see-<u>ohn</u> deh koh-<u>reh</u>-oh
eh-lek-<u>troh</u>-nee-koh

. . . your (cell) phone number?
. . . tu número de teléfono (celular/móvil)?
too <u>noo</u>-mehr-oh deh teh-<u>leh</u>-foh-noh (seh-loo-lar/<u>moh</u>-veel)

529. My e-mail address is . . .
Mi dirección de correo electrónico es . . .
Mee dee-rek-see-<u>ohn</u> deh koh-<u>reh</u>-oh eh-lek-<u>troh</u>-nee-koh ess

530. My (cell) phone number is . . .
Mi número de teléfono (celular/móvil) es . . .
Mee <u>noo</u>-meh-roh deh teh-<u>leh</u>-foh-noh (seh-loo-<u>lar</u>/<u>moh</u>-veel)
ess

531. Call me.   *Llámame.*   <u>Yah</u>-mah-meh

532. It's (always) busy.   *(Siempre) Está ocupado.*
(See-<u>em</u>-preh) Ess-<u>tah</u> oh-koo-<u>pah</u>-doh

533. There's a lot of interference.   *Hay mucha interferencia.*
I <u>moo</u>-chah een-tehr-feh-<u>ren</u>-see-ah

534. I can't hear you. (inf.)   *No te escucho.*
Noh teh ess-<u>koo</u>-choh

535. Speak louder. (inf.)   *Habla más fuerte.*
<u>Ah</u>-blah mahss <u>fwehr</u>-teh

536. I can't speak any louder.   *No puedo hablar más fuerte.*
No <u>pweh</u>-doh ah-<u>blar</u> mahss <u>fwehr</u>-teh

537. The call was cut off.   *Se cortó la llamada.*
Seh kor-<u>toh</u> lah yah-<u>mah</u>-dah

538. Wrong number.   *El número está equivocado.*
El <u>noo</u>-meh-roh ess-<u>tah</u> eh-kee-voh-<u>kah</u>-doh

539. Who's speaking?   *¿Quién habla?*   Kee-<u>en</u> <u>ah</u>-blah

540. May I speak to . . . ?   *¿Puedo hablar con . . . ?*
<u>Pweh</u>-doh ah-<u>blar</u> kohn

541. Is . . . there?   *¿Está . . . ahí?*   Ess-<u>tah</u> . . . ah-<u>ee</u>

542. My name is . . .   *Mi nombre es . . .*
Mee <u>nohm</u>-breh ess . . .

543. Do you know at what time he/she'll be back? (for.)
¿Sabe a qué hora vuelve?   Sah-beh ah keh oh-rah vwel-veh

544. Please tell him/her I called. (for.)   *Por favor dígale que llamé.*
Por fah-vor dee-gah-leh keh yah-meh

545. Please tell him/her to call me back. (for.)
Por favor dígale que me llame.
Por fah-vor dee-gah-leh keh meh yah-meh

546. As soon as he/she gets there.   *En cuanto llegue.*
En kwahn-toh yeh-geh

547. He/she has my number.   *Él/ella tiene mi número.*
El/Eh-yah tee-eh-neh mee noo-meh-roh

548. I will call later.   *Llamaré más tarde.*
Yah-mah-reh mahss tar-deh

549. It's (not) (very) important.   *(No) es (muy) importante.*
(Noh) ess (mooy) eem-por-tahn-teh

550. I tried calling you several times. (inf.)
Traté de llamarte varias veces.
Trah-teh deh yah-mar-teh vah-ree-ahss veh-sess

551. Where were you? (inf.)   *¿Dónde estabas?*
Dohn-deh ess-tah-bahss

552. Did you get my message? (inf.)
¿Recibiste mi recado?   Reh-see-bees-teh mee reh-kah-doh

553. Do you have a phone book? (for.)
¿Tiene un directorio telefónico?
Tee-eh-neh oon dee-rek-toh-ree-oh teh-leh-foh-nee-koh
. . . the yellow pages?   *. . . la sección amarilla?*
lah sek-see-ohn ah-mah-ree-yah

554. I need to look up a number/an address.
Necesito buscar un número/una dirección.
Neh-seh-see-toh boos-kahr oon noo-meh-roh/oo-nah
dee-rek-see-ohn

555. I'm looking for an Internet café (with Macs).
Estoy buscando un cibercafé (con Macs).
Ess-**toy** boos **kahn**-doh oon see behr-kah-**feh** (kohn Macs)

 . . . a public phone. . . . *un teléfono público.*
oon teh-**leh**-foh-noh **poo**-blee-koh

556. What's the rate per minute? *¿Cuál es la tarifa por minuto?*
Kwahl ess lah tah-**ree**-fah por mee-**noo**-toh

 . . . per quarter of an hour? . . . *por un cuarto de hora?*
por oon **kwar**-toh de **oh**-rah

 . . . per hour? . . . *por hora?* por **oh**-rah

557. Can I print a document? *¿Puedo imprimir un documento?*
Pweh-doh eem-pree-**meer** oon doh-koo-**men**-toh

558. How do I scan these pages? *¿Cómo escaneo estas páginas?*
Koh-moh ess-kah-**neh**-oh **ess**-tahss **pah**-hee-nahss

559. Help me make a photocopy. (for.)
Ayúdeme a hacer una fotocopia.
Ah-**yoo**-deh-meh ah ah-**sehr** **oo**-nah foh-toh-**koh**-pee-ah

560. How much is it per page? *¿Cuánto cuesta por página?*
Kwahn-toh **kwess**-tah por **pah**-hee-nah

RELIGIOUS SERVICES

561. I'm an atheist. *Soy ateo.* Soy ah-**teh**-oh
 . . . Ba'hai. . . . *ba'hai.* **bah**-hai
 . . . Buddhist. . . . *budista.* boo-**dees**-tah
 . . . Catholic. . . . *católico.* kah-**toh**-lee-koh
 . . . Christian. . . . *cristiano.* krees-tee-**ah**-noh
 . . . Jewish. . . . *judío.* hoo-**dee**-oh
 . . . Muslim. . . . *Musulmán.* moo-sool-**mahn**

562. Where is the church? *¿Dónde está la iglesia?*
Dohn-deh ess-**tah** lah ee-**gleh**-see-ah

 . . . the mosque? . . . *la mezquita?* lah mess-**kee**-tah

 . . . the synagogue? . . . *la sinagoga?*
lah see-nah-**goh**-gah

 . . . the temple? . . . *el templo?* el **tem**-ploh

563. At what time are services held?
¿A qué hora son los servicios?
Ah keh <u>oh</u>-rah sohn lohss sehr-<u>vee</u>-see-ohss

564. May I speak to the imam?   *¿Puedo hablar con el imam?*
<u>Pweh</u>-doh ah-<u>blar</u> kohn el <u>ee</u>-mahm

. . . the pastor?   . . . *el pastor?*   **el pahss-<u>tor</u>**

. . . the priest?   . . . *el cura?*   **el <u>koo</u>-rah**

. . . the rabbi?   . . . *el rabino?*   **el rah-<u>bee</u>-noh**

CULTURE & ENTERTAINMENT

565. Let's go to the (contemporary) art museum.
Vamos al museo de arte (contemporáneo).
**<u>Vah</u>-mohss ahl moo-<u>seh</u>-oh deh <u>ar</u>-teh
kohn-tem-por-<u>ah</u>-neh-oh**

. . . archaeology museum.   . . . *museo de arqueología.*
moo-<u>seh</u>-oh deh ar-keh-oh-loh-<u>gee</u>-ah

. . . the craft museum.   . . . *museo de artesanías.*
moo-<u>seh</u>-oh deh ar-teh-sah-<u>nee</u>-ahss

. . . the natural history museum.
. . . *museo de historia natural.*
moo-<u>seh</u>-oh deh ees-<u>toh</u>-ree-ah nah-too-<u>rahl</u>

566. At what time does it open/close?   *¿A qué hora abre/cierra?*
Ah keh <u>oh</u>-rah <u>ah</u>-breh/see-<u>eh</u>-rah

567. Is it free on Thursdays?   *¿Es gratis los jueves?*
Ess <u>grah</u>-tees lohss <u>hweh</u>-vess

568. Is there a discount for students/teachers?
¿Hay descuento para estudiantes/profesores?
I des-<u>kwen</u>-toh <u>pah</u>-rah ess-too-dee-<u>ahn</u>-tess/proh-feh-<u>soh</u>-ress

. . . for children?   . . . *para niños?*   **<u>pah</u>-rah <u>nee</u>-nyohss**

. . . for the elderly?   . . . *para ancianos?*
<u>pah</u>-rah ahn-see-<u>ah</u>-nohss

569. Is it handicap-accessible?   *¿Hay acceso para minusválidos?*
I ahk-<u>seh</u>-soh <u>pah</u>-rah mee-noos-<u>vahl</u>-ee-dohss

570. I'm interested in the painting exhibition.
      Me interesa la exposición de pintura.
      Meh een-tehr-<u>eh</u>-sah lah eks-poh-see see-<u>ohn</u> deh peen-<u>too</u>-rah

      . . . the sculpture exhibition.   . . . *la exposición de escultura.*
      lah eks-poh-see-see-<u>ohn</u> deh ess-kool-<u>too</u>-rah

      . . . the pre-Hispanic art exhibition.
      . . . *la exposición de arte prehispánico.*
      lah eks-poh-see-see-<u>ohn</u> deh <u>ar</u>-teh preh-ees-<u>pah</u>-nee-koh

571. We want to take a guided tour of the museum.
      Queremos una visita guiada del museo.
      Keh-<u>reh</u>-mohss <u>oo</u>-nah vee-<u>see</u>-tah gee-<u>ah</u>-dah del moo-<u>seh</u>-oh

      . . . of the city.   . . . *de la ciudad.*   deh lah <u>see</u>-oo-dahd

572. Is (flash) photography allowed?
      ¿Se permite tomar fotografías (con flash)?
      Seh pehr-<u>mee</u>-teh toh-<u>mar</u> foh-toh-grah-<u>fee</u>-ahss (kohn flash)

573. Don't you all want to go to the movies?
      ¿No quieren ir al cine?   Noh kee-<u>eh</u>-ren eer ahl <u>see</u>-neh

574. Which direction is the theatre?   *¿Hacia dónde está el teatro?*
      Ah-<u>see</u>-yah <u>dohn</u>-deh ess-<u>tah</u> el teh-<u>ah</u>-troh

575. What's playing?   *¿Qué hay en la cartelera?*
      Keh I en lah kar-teh-<u>leh</u>-rah

576. At what time is the show?   *¿A qué hora es la función?*
      Ah keh <u>oh</u>-rah ess lah foon-see-<u>ohn</u>

577. How long is the show?   *¿Cuánto dura la función?*
      <u>Kwahn</u>-toh <u>doo</u>-rah lah foon-see-<u>ohn</u>

578. How much are the tickets?
      ¿Cuánto cuestan los boletos/las entradas?
      <u>Kwahn</u>-toh <u>kwess</u>-tahn lohss boh-<u>leh</u>-tohss/lahss
      en-<u>trah</u>-dahss

579. Is the movie dubbed in Spanish?
      ¿Está doblada al español la película?
      Ess-<u>tah</u> doh-<u>blah</u>-dah ahl ess-pah-<u>nyohl</u> lah peh-<u>lee</u>-koo-lah

580.   Did you like the movie/the play?
       ¿Te gustó la película/la obra?
       Teh goos-<u>toh</u> lah peh-<u>lee</u>-koo-lah/lah <u>oh</u>-brah

581.   I liked it (a lot).   *Me gustó (mucho).*
       Meh goos-<u>toh</u> (<u>moo</u>-choh)

582.   I didn't like it (at all).   *No me gustó (nada).*
       Noh meh goos-<u>toh</u> (<u>nah</u>-dah)

583.   What's your favorite movie?   *¿Cuál es tu película favorita?*
       Kwahl ess too peh-<u>lee</u>-koo-lah fah-voh-<u>ree</u>-tah

584.   I feel like going dancing.   *Tengo ganas de ir a bailar.*
       <u>Ten</u>-goh <u>gah</u>-nahss deh eer ah bi-<u>lar</u>

       . . . partying.   . . . *ir de fiesta.*   eer deh fee-<u>ess</u>-tah

       . . . bar hopping. (Sp.)   . . . *ir de marcha.*
       eer deh <u>mar</u>-chah

585.   Do you like to dance? (inf.)   *¿Te gusta bailar?*
       Teh <u>goos</u>-tah bi-<u>lar</u>

586.   Can we go to a (rock/classical music) concert?
       ¿Podemos ir a un concierto (de rock/música clásica)?
       Poh-<u>deh</u>-mohss eer ah oon kohn-see-<u>ehr</u>-toh (de rock/<u>moo</u>-
       see-kah <u>klahss</u>-see-kah)

       . . . to a fun place?   . . . *ir a un lugar divertido?*
       eer ah oon loo-<u>gar</u> dee-vehr-<u>tee</u>-doh

       . . . to a nightclub?
       . . . *ir a un club nocturno/una discoteca?*
       eer ah oon kloob nohk-<u>toor</u>-noh/<u>oo</u>-nah dees-koh-<u>teh</u>-kah

       . . . to a gay bar?   . . . *ir a un bar gay?*
       eer ah oon bar gay

587.   Where can we go?   *¿A dónde podemos ir?*
       Ah <u>dohn</u>-deh poh-<u>deh</u>-mohss eer

588.   What's the cover charge?   *¿Cuánto cuesta la entrada?*
       <u>Kwahn</u>-toh <u>kwess</u>-tah lah en-<u>trah</u>-dah

589.   Do I need to take an ID?
       ¿Necesito llevar una identificación?
       Neh-seh-<u>see</u>-toh yeh-<u>vahr</u> <u>oo</u>-nah ee-den-tee-fee-kah-see-<u>ohn</u>

590. I'm over eighteen years old. *Soy mayor de dieciocho años.*
Soy mah-<u>yor</u> deh dee-eh-see-<u>oh</u>-choh <u>ah</u>-nyohss.

591. I (don't) drink alcohol. *(No) Bebo alcohol.*
(Noh) <u>Beh</u>-boh ahl-<u>kohl</u>

592. I (don't) like drugs. *(No)Me gustan las drogas.*
(Noh) Meh <u>goos</u>-tahn lahss <u>droh</u>-gahss

593. We are (not) going out tonight.
(No) Vamos a salir esta noche.
(Noh) <u>Vah</u>-mohss ah sah-<u>leer</u> <u>ess</u>-tah <u>noh</u>-cheh

594. We have other plans this weekend.
Tenemos otros planes este fin de semana.
Teh-<u>neh</u>-mohss <u>oh</u>-trohss <u>plah</u>-nehss <u>ess</u>-teh feen deh
seh-<u>mah</u>-nah

595. Do you want to go with me? (inf.) *¿Quieres ir conmigo?*
Kee-<u>eh</u>-ress eer kohn-<u>mee</u>-goh

596. Would you like to dance with me? (inf.)
¿Quieres bailar conmigo? Kee-<u>eh</u>-ress bi-<u>lar</u> kohn-<u>mee</u>-goh

597. I can't dance (but I don't care).
No sé bailar (pero no me importa).
Noh seh bi-<u>lar</u> (<u>peh</u>-roh noh meh eem-<u>por</u>-tah)

   . . . sing.   . . . *cantar.*   kahn-<u>tar</u>

598. At what time shall we meet? *¿A qué hora nos vemos?*
Ah keh <u>oh</u>-rah nohss <u>veh</u>-mohss

599. Where shall we meet? *¿Dónde nos vemos?*
<u>Dohn</u>-deh nohss <u>veh</u>-mohss

600. We will meet at the entrance. *Nos vemos en la entrada.*
Nohss <u>veh</u>-mohss en lah en-<u>trah</u>-dah

601. Can you pick us up? (inf.) *¿Puedes pasar a recogernos?*
<u>Pweh</u>-dess pah-<u>sar</u> ah reh-koh-<u>hehr</u>-nohss

602. Party on! *¡Que siga la fiesta!* Keh <u>see</u>-gah lah fee-<u>ess</u>-tah

603. This is fun/boring. *Esto está muy divertido/aburrido.*
<u>Ess</u>-toh ess-<u>tah</u> mooy dee-vehr-<u>tee</u>-doh/ah-boo-<u>ree</u>-doh

604. Let's go somewhere else.   *Vamos a otro lado.*
     <u>Vah</u>-mohss ah <u>oh</u>-troh <u>lah</u>-doh

605. Party's over.   *Se acabó la fiesta.*
     Seh ah-kah-<u>boh</u> lah fee-<u>ess</u>-tah

606. It's time to go home (to sleep).
     Es hora de ir a casa (a dormir).
     Ess <u>oh</u>-rah deh eer ah <u>kah</u>-sah (ah dor-<u>meer</u>)

607. I detest hangovers.   *Detesto las crudas/resacas. (Sp.)*
     Deh-<u>tess</u>-toh lahss <u>kroo</u>-dahss/reh-<u>sah</u>-kahss

MONEY & SHOPPING

608. I need to change currencies.   *Necesito cambiar dinero.*
     Neh-seh-<u>see</u>-toh kahm-bee-<u>ar</u> dee-<u>neh</u>-roh

609. I have to buy some traveler's checks.
     Tengo que comprar unos cheques de viajero.
     <u>Ten</u>-goh keh kohm-<u>prar</u> <u>oo</u>-nohss <u>cheh</u>-kess deh
     vee-ah-<u>heh</u>-roh

610. Where is there a bank?   *¿Dónde hay un banco?*
     <u>Dohn</u>-deh I oon <u>bahn</u>-koh

611. Is there a currency exchange office around here?
     ¿Hay una casa de cambio por aquí?
     I <u>oo</u>-nah <u>kah</u>-sah deh <u>kahm</u>-bee-oh por ah-<u>kee</u>

612. What's the exchange rate?   *¿Cuál es el tipo de cambio?*
     Kwahl ess el <u>tee</u>-poh deh <u>kahm</u>-bee-oh

613. Do I have to pay a commission?
     ¿Hay que pagar una comisión?
     I keh pah-<u>gar</u> <u>oo</u>-nah koh-mee-see-<u>ohn</u>

614. Give me small bills, please. (for.)
     Deme billetes pequeños, por favor.
     <u>Deh</u>-meh bee-<u>yeh</u>-tess peh-<u>keh</u>-nyohss, por fah-<u>vor</u>

615. Can you give me a receipt?   *¿Me puede dar un recibo?*
     Meh <u>pweh</u>-deh dar oon reh-<u>see</u>-boh

616. Let's go to an ATM.   *Vamos a un cajero automático.*
<u>Vah</u>-mohss ah oon kah-<u>heh</u>-roh ow-toh-<u>mah</u>-tee-koh

617. Our budget is (very) limited.
Nuestro presupuesto es (muy) limitado.
<u>Nwess</u>-troh preh-soo-<u>pwess</u>-toh ess (mooy) lee-mee-<u>tah</u>-doh

618. We (don't) have a lot of money.
(No) Tenemos (mucho) dinero.
(Noh) Teh-<u>neh</u>-mohss <u>moo</u>-choh dee-<u>neh</u>-roh

619. We (don't) want to spend a lot.
(No) Queremos gastar mucho.
(Noh) Keh-<u>reh</u>-mohss gahss-<u>tahr</u> <u>moo</u>-choh

620. I want to go to a clothing store.
Quiero ir a una tienda de ropa.
Kee-<u>eh</u>-roh eer ah <u>oo</u>-nah tee-<u>en</u>-dah deh <u>roh</u>-pah

. . . shoe store.   . . . *una tienda de zapatos/zapatería.*
<u>oo</u>-nah tee-<u>en</u>-dah deh sah-<u>pah</u>-tohss/sah-pah-teh-<u>ree</u>-ah

. . . a handicrafts store.   . . . *una tienda de artesanías.*
<u>oo</u>-nah tee-<u>en</u>-dah deh ar-teh-sah-<u>nee</u>-ahss

. . . a traditional market.   . . . *a un mercado típico.*
ah oon mehr-<u>kah</u>-doh <u>tee</u>-pee-koh

. . . a shopping mall.   . . . *un centro comercial.*
oon <u>sen</u>-troh koh-mehr-see-<u>ahl</u>

. . . an antique store.   . . . *una tienda de antigüedades.*
<u>oo</u>-nah tee-<u>en</u>-dah deh ahn-tee-weh-<u>dah</u>-dess

. . . a gallery.   . . . *una galería.*   <u>oo</u>-nah gah-leh-<u>ree</u>-ah

. . . a jewelry store.   . . . *una joyería.*
<u>oo</u>-nah hoy-eh-<u>ree</u>-ah

621. Do you know where I can find a (used, English) book store?
¿Sabe dónde puedo encontrar una librería (de libros usados, en inglés)?
<u>Sah</u>-beh <u>dohn</u>-deh <u>pweh</u>-doh en-kohn-<u>trar</u> <u>oo</u>-nah
lee-breh-<u>ree</u>-ah (deh <u>lee</u>-brohss oo-<u>sah</u>-dohss, en-een-<u>gless</u>)

. . . an office-supply store?   . . . *una papelería?*
<u>oo</u>-nah pah-pel-eh-<u>ree</u>-ah

. . . a hardware store?   . . . *una ferretería?*
<u>oo</u>-nah fehr-reh-teh-<u>ree</u>-ah

622. Where can I buy souvenirs?
      ¿Dónde puedo comprar recuerdos?
      <u>Dohn</u>-deh <u>pweh</u>-doh kohm-<u>prar</u> reh-<u>kwehr</u>-dohss

623. At what time do they open/close?
      ¿A qué hora abren/cierran?
      Ah keh <u>oh</u>-rah <u>ah</u>-bren/see-<u>eh</u>-ran

624. Just browsing, thank you.   *Sólo estoy mirando, gracias.*
      <u>Soh</u>-loh ess-<u>toy</u> mee-<u>rahn</u>-doh, <u>grah</u>-see-ahss

625. Can I look at it?   *¿Puedo verlo?*   <u>Pweh</u>-doh <u>vehr</u>-loh

626. (Where) Can I try this on?   *¿(Dónde) Puedo probarme esto?*
      (<u>Dohn</u>-deh) <u>Pweh</u>-doh proh-<u>bar</u>-meh <u>ess</u>-toh

627. It's too big/small.   *Me queda grande/chico.*
      Meh <u>keh</u>-dah <u>grahn</u>-deh/<u>chee</u>-koh

628. I need a bigger/smaller size.
      Necesito una talla más grande/chica.
      Neh-seh-<u>see</u>-toh <u>oo</u>-nah <u>tah</u>-yah mahss <u>grahn</u>-deh/<u>chee</u>-kah

629. Do you have more like this one? (for.)
      ¿Tiene más como éste?   Tee-<u>eh</u>-neh mahss <u>koh</u>-moh <u>ess</u>-teh

630. I want another one like it.   *Quiero otro igual.*
      Kee-<u>eh</u>-roh <u>oh</u>-troh ee-<u>wahl</u>

631. Do you have other colors/models?
      ¿Tiene otros colores/modelos?
      Tee-<u>eh</u>-neh <u>oh</u>-trohss koh-<u>loh</u>-ress/moh-<u>deh</u>-lohss

      . . . a mirror?   . . . *un espejo?*   oon ess-<u>peh</u>-hoh

632. How much does this cost?   *¿Cuánto cuesta/vale esto?*
      <u>Kwahn</u>-toh <u>kwess</u>-tah/<u>vah</u>-leh <u>ess</u>-toh

633. What's the price of that?   *¿Qué precio tiene eso?*
      Keh <u>preh</u>-see-oh tee-<u>en</u>-eh <u>eh</u>-soh

634. It's free.   *Es gratis.*   Ess <u>grah</u>-tees

635. It's very expensive/cheap.   *Es muy caro/barato.*
      Ess mooy <u>kah</u>-roh/bah-<u>rah</u>-toh

636. It's too much.   *Es demasiado.*   **Ess deh-mah-see-ah-doh**

637. I'm looking for something cheaper
Estoy buscando algo más barato.
Ess-toy boos-kahn-doh ahl-goh mahss bah-rah-toh

     . . . of better quality.   . . . *de mejor calidad.*
deh meh-hor kah-lee-dahd

     . . . specific.   . . . *en particular.*   **en par-tee-koo-lar**

638. Can you give me a good/better price? (for.)
¿Me puede dar un buen/mejor precio?
Meh pweh-deh dar oon bwen/meh-hor preh-see-oh

639. I can't pay so much.   *No puedo pagar tanto.*
Noh pweh-doh pah-gar tahn-toh

640. I don't have enough money.   *No me alcanza el dinero.*
Noh meh ahl-kahn-sah el dee-neh-roh

641. It has a twenty percent discount.
Tiene un descuento del veinte por ciento.
Tee-eh-neh oon dess-kwen-toh del vayn-teh por see-en-toh

642. It's on sale.   *Está de rebaja.*   **Ess-tah deh reh-bah-hah**

643. I'll take it.   *Me lo llevo.*   **Meh loh yeh-voh**

644. Does it have a warranty?   *¿Tiene garantía?*
Tee-eh-neh gah-rahn-tee-ah

645. Where do I pay?   *¿Dónde se paga?*
Dohn-deh seh pah-gah

646. Do you accept credit cards?   *¿Aceptan tarjetas de crédito?*
Ah-sep-tahn tar-heh-tahss deh kreh-dee-toh

     . . . debit cards?   . . . *tarjetas de débito?*
tar-heh-tahss deh deh-bee-toh

     . . . American dollars?   . . . *dólares americanos?*
doh-lah-ress ah-meh-ree-kah-nohss

647. Can I return it?   *¿Puedo devolverlo?*
Pweh-doh deh-vohl-vehr-loh

648. I need a receipt.   *Necesito un recibo.*
Neh-seh-see-toh oon reh-see-boh

649. Can you (gift) wrap it? (for.)
 ¿*Lo puede envolver (para regalo)?*
 Loh <u>pweh</u>-deh en-vohl-<u>vehr</u> (<u>pah</u>-rah reh-<u>gah</u>-loh)

650. Can you put it in a bag/box?   ¿*Lo puede poner en una bolsa/
 caja?*   Loh <u>pweh</u>-deh poh-<u>nehr</u> en <u>oo</u>-nah <u>bol</u>-sah/<u>kah</u>-hah

651. It's broken. [in pieces].   *Está roto.*   Ess-<u>tah</u> <u>roh</u>-toh

652. It's broken. [it does not work].   *Está descompuesto.*
 Ess-<u>tah</u> dess-kohm-<u>pwes</u>-toh

653. I believe it's defective.   *Creo que está defectuoso.*
 <u>Kreh</u>-oh keh ess-<u>tah</u> deh-fek-<u>twoh</u>-soh

654. It doesn't work.   *No funciona.*   Noh foon-see-<u>oh</u>-nah

655. I want to return it.   *Quiero devolverlo.*
 Kee-<u>eh</u>-roh deh-vohl-<u>vehr</u>-loh

656. I need a replacement.   *Necesito una substitución.*
 Neh-seh-<u>see</u>-toh <u>oo</u>-nah soob-stee-too-see-<u>ohn</u>

657. Please give me a refund.   *Por favor deme un reembolso.*
 Por fah-<u>vor</u> deh-meh oon ray-em-<u>bol</u>-soh

REST & RELAXATION

658. I can't go on.   *No puedo seguir.*   Noh <u>pweh</u>-doh seh-<u>geer</u>
 . . . walk anymore.   . . . *caminar más.*
 kah-mee-<u>nar</u> mahss

659. I'm too tired.   *Estoy demasiado cansado.*
 Ess-<u>toy</u> deh-mah-see-<u>ah</u>-doh kahn-<u>sah</u>-doh

660. I need to rest (a bit).   *Necesito descansar (un poco).*
 Neh-seh-<u>see</u>-toh dess-kahn-<u>sar</u> (oon <u>poh</u>-koh)
 . . . sit in the shade.   . . . *sentarme a la sombra.*
 sen-<u>tar</u>-meh ah lah <u>sohm</u>-brah
 . . . lie down in a hammock.
 . . . *acostarme en una hamaca.*
 ah-kohs-<u>tar</u>-meh en <u>oo</u>-nah ah-<u>mah</u>-kah

661. I want to sunbathe by the pool.
      Quiero asolearme junto a la alberca.
      Kee-<u>eh</u>-roh ah-soh-leh-<u>ar</u>-meh <u>hoon</u> toh ah lah ahl-<u>behr</u>-kah

      . . . take a nap.   . . . *dormir una siesta.*
      dor-<u>meer</u> <u>oo</u>-nah see-<u>ess</u>-tah

662. I just want to relax.   *Sólo quiero relajarme.*
      <u>Soh</u>-loh kee-<u>eh</u>-roh reh-lah-<u>har</u>-meh

663. I don't want to do anything.   *No quiero hacer nada.*
      Noh kee-<u>eh</u>-roh ah-<u>sehr</u> <u>nah</u>-dah

664. I don't feel like doing anything.
      No tengo ganas de hacer nada.
      Noh <u>ten</u>-goh <u>gah</u>-nahss de ah-<u>sehr</u> <u>nah</u>-dah

665. I don't need to visit any more places.
      No necesito visitar más lugares.
      Noh neh-seh-<u>see</u>-toh vee-see-<u>tar</u> mahss loo-<u>gar</u>-ess

666. I would rather not go out tonight.
      Preferiría no salir esta noche.
      Preh-feh-ree-<u>ree</u>-ah noh sah-<u>leer</u> <u>ess</u>-tah <u>noh</u>-cheh

667. Can we stay here?   *¿Podemos quedarnos aquí?*
      Poh-<u>deh</u>-mohss keh-<u>dar</u>-nohss ah-<u>kee</u>

668. I'm fed up.   *Ya estoy harto.*   Yah ess-<u>toy</u> <u>ar</u>-toh

669. I just want to watch a little TV.
      Sólo quiero ver un poco de televisión.
      <u>Soh</u>-loh kee-<u>eh</u>-roh vehr oon <u>poh</u>-koh deh teh-leh-vee-see-<u>ohn</u>

      . . . read a book.   . . . *leer un libro.*   lay-<u>ehr</u> oon <u>lee</u>-broh

670. We could play cards.   *Podríamos jugar a las cartas.*
      Poh-<u>dree</u>-ah-mohss hoo-<u>gar</u> ah lahss <u>kar</u>-tahss

      . . . video games.   . . . *video juegos.*
      <u>vee</u>-deh-oh <u>hweh</u>-gohss

      . . . a board game.   . . . *un juego de mesa.*
      oon <u>hweh</u>-goh deh <u>meh</u>-sah

671. We can rent a movie.   *Podemos rentar una película.*
      Poh-<u>deh</u>-mohss ren-<u>tar</u> <u>oo</u>-nah peh-<u>lee</u>-koo-lah

. . . listen to music.   . . . *escuchar música*.
ess-koo-<u>char</u> <u>moo</u>-see-kah

. . . talk for a while.   . . . *platicar un rato*.
plah-tee-<u>kar</u> oon <u>rah</u>-toh

. . . meditate in silence.   . . . *meditar en silencio*.
meh-dee-<u>tar</u> en see-<u>len</u>-see-oh

672. I would rather have dinner at home.   *Prefiero cenar en casa*.
Preh-fee-<u>eh</u>-roh seh-<u>nar</u> en <u>kah</u>-sah

673. I would like to take a hot bath.
Me gustaría tomar un baño caliente.
Meh goos-tah-<u>ree</u>-ah toh-<u>mar</u> oon <u>bah</u>-nyoh kah-lee-<u>en</u>-teh

. . . go to bed early.   . . . *acostarme temprano*.
ah-kohs-<u>tar</u>-meh tem-<u>prah</u>-noh

674. I hope to sleep for twelve hours.
Espero dormir por doce horas.
Ess-<u>peh</u>-roh dor-<u>meer</u> por <u>doh</u>-seh <u>oh</u>-rahss

675. I'm exhausted.   *Estoy exhausto*.
Ess-toy eks-<u>ow</u>-stoh

676. Don't wake me up.   *No me despiertes*.
Noh meh dess-pee-<u>ehr</u>-tess

677. I don't want to be bothered.   *No quiero que me molesten*.
Noh kee-<u>eh</u>-roh keh meh moh-<u>less</u>-ten

678. Tomorrow will be another day.   *Mañana será otro día*.
Mah-<u>nyah</u>-nah seh-<u>rah</u> <u>oh</u>-troh <u>dee</u>-ah

COMPUTERS & INTERNET

679. I need to use a computer.   *Necesito usar una computadora*.
Neh-seh-<u>see</u>-toh oo-<u>sar</u> <u>oo</u>-nah kohm-poo-tah-<u>doh</u>-rah

. . . a computer.   . . . *un ordenador. (Sp.)*
oon or-deh-nah-<u>dor</u>

680. Where can I connect to the Internet?
¿Dónde puedo conectarme a la red?
<u>Dohn</u>-deh <u>pweh</u>-doh koh-nek-<u>tar</u>-meh ah lah red?

681.   Do you have a laptop computer? (inf.)
       ¿Tienes una computadora portátil?
       Tee-**eh**-ness **oo**-nah kohm-poo-tah-**doh**-rah por-**tah**-teel

       . . . a laptop computer?   . . . *un ordenador portátil? (Sp.)*
       oon or-deh-nah-**dor** por-**tah**-teel

682.   Is it a Mac or a PC?   *¿Es una Mac o una PC?*
       Ess **oo**-nah Mac oh **oo**-nah peh-**seh**

683.   I don't know the keyboard shortcuts.
       No conozco los atajos del teclado.
       Noh koh-**nohss**-koh lohss ah-**tah**-hohss del teh-**klah**-doh

684.   I do everything with the mouse.   *Lo hago todo con el ratón.*
       Loh **ah**-goh **toh**-doh kohn el rah-**tohn**

685.   What happens if I click on this icon?
       ¿Qué pasa si hago clic en este icono?
       Keh **pah**-sah see **ah**-goh kleek en **ess**-teh ee-**koh**-noh

686.   How can I get on-line?
       ¿Cómo puedo conectarme a la red?
       Koh-moh **pweh**-doh koh-nek-**tar**-meh ah lah red

       . . . get off-line?   . . . *desconectarme de la red?*
       dess-koh-nek-**tar**-meh deh lah red

687.   I would like to check my e-mail.
       Quisiera revisar mi correo electrónico.
       Kee-see-**eh**-rah reh-vee-**sar** mee koh-**reh**-oh
       eh-lek-**troh**-nee-koh

       . . . send an e-mail.
       . . . *enviar/mandar un correo electrónico.*
       en-vee-**ahr**/mahn-**dar** oon koh-**reh**-oh eh-lek-**troh**-nee-koh

688.   My e-mail address is . . .   *Mi dirección electrónica es . . .*
       Mee dee-rek-see-**ohn** eh-lek-**troh**-nee-kah ess

689.   It's iluvspanish@[at] mymail.[dot] com.
       Es iluvspanish@ [arroba] mymail.[punto] com.
       Ess iluvspanish ah-**roh**-bah mymail **poon**-toh com

690.   What's the name of the website?
       ¿Cómo se llama el sitio electrónico?
       Koh-moh seh **yah**-mah el **see**-tee-oh eh-lek-**troh**-nee-koh

691.   First, open the browser. (inf.)   *Primero, abre el navegador.*
Pree-<u>meh</u>-roh <u>ah</u>-breh el nah-veh-gah-<u>dohr</u>

692.   You can use the desktop shortcut. (inf.)
Puedes usar el acceso directo en el escritorio.
<u>Pweh</u>-dess oo-<u>sar</u> el ahk-<u>seh</u>-soh dee-<u>rek</u>-toh en el
ess-kree-<u>toh</u>-ree-oh

693.   Now we can surf through cyberspace.
Ahora podemos navegar por el ciberespacio.
Ah-<u>oh</u>-rah po-<u>deh</u>-mohss nah-veh-<u>gar</u> por el
see-behr-ess-<u>pah</u>-see-oh

694.   Search for the webpage. (inf.)   *Busca la página electrónica.*
<u>Boos</u>-kah lah <u>pah</u>-hee-nah eh-lek-<u>troh</u>-nee-kah

695.   What's your favorite search engine? (inf.)
¿Cuál es tu buscador favorito?
Kwahl ess too boos-kah-<u>dohr</u> fah-voh-<u>ree</u>-toh

696.   I want to go to the site's home page.
Quiero ir a la página principal del sitio.
Kee-<u>eh</u>-roh eer ah lah <u>pah</u>-hee-nah preen-see-<u>pahl</u> del
<u>see</u>-tee-oh

697.   Click on the link. (inf.)   *Haz clic en el enlace.*
Ahss kleek en el en-<u>lah</u>-seh

698.   My username is . . .   *Mi nombre de usuario es . . .*
Mee <u>nohm</u>-breh deh oo-<u>swah</u>-ree-oh ess

699.   What's the password?   *¿Cuál es la contraseña?*
Kwahl ess lah kohn-trah-<u>seh</u>-nyah

700.   I have too much spam/junk mail.
Tengo demasiado correo basura.
<u>Ten</u>-goh deh-mah-see-<u>ah</u>-doh koh-<u>reh</u>-oh bah-<u>soo</u>-rah

701.   I want to edit the message.   *Quiero editar el mensaje.*
Kee-<u>eh</u>-roh eh-dee-<u>tar</u> el men-<u>sah</u>-heh

. . . copy and paste this word.
. . . copiar y pegar esta palabra.
koh-pee-<u>ar</u> ee peh-<u>gar</u> <u>ess</u>-tah pah-<u>lah</u>-brah

. . . cut and paste these lines.
. . *cortar y pegar estas líneas.*
kor-<u>tar</u> ee peh-<u>gar</u> <u>ess</u>-tahss <u>lee</u>-neh-alıss

. . . delete this section.   . . *borrar esta sección.*
boh-<u>rar</u> <u>ess</u>-tah sek-see-<u>ohn</u>

702. I need to save the document to the hard disk.
Necesito guardar el documento en el disco duro.
Neh-seh-<u>see</u>-toh gwar-<u>dar</u> el doh-koo-<u>men</u>-toh en el <u>dees</u>-koh <u>doo</u>-roh

. . . save it in a new folder.
. . . *guardarlo en una carpeta nueva.*
gwar-<u>dar</u>-loh en <u>oo</u>-nah kar-<u>peh</u>-tah <u>nweh</u>-vah

. . . save it as a PDF.   . . . *guardarlo como un PDF.*
gwar-<u>dar</u>-loh <u>koh</u>-moh oon peh deh <u>eh</u>-feh

703. Is it possible to print it from here?
¿Es posible imprimirlo desde aquí?
Ess poh-<u>see</u>-bleh eem-pree-<u>meer</u>-loh <u>dess</u>-deh ah-<u>kee</u>

704. The printer is running out of ink/toner.
Se le está acabando la tinta/el toner a la impresora.
Seh leh ess-<u>tah</u> ah-kah-<u>bahn</u>-doh lah <u>teen</u>-tah/el toh-<u>nehr</u> ah lah eem-preh-<u>soh</u>-rah

705. The paper jammed.   *Se atoró el papel.*
Seh ah-toh-<u>roh</u> el pah-<u>pel</u>

706. I'm missing some pages.   *Me faltan algunas páginas.*
Meh <u>fahl</u>-tahn ahl-<u>goo</u>-nahss <u>pah</u>-hee-nahss

707. Can I attach a file?   *¿Puedo adjuntar un archivo?*
<u>Pweh</u>-doh ahd-hoon-<u>tar</u> oon ahr-<u>chee</u>-voh

708. How do I open the attached file?
¿Cómo abro el archivo adjunto?
<u>Koh</u>-moh <u>ah</u>-broh el ahr-<u>chee</u>-voh ahd-<u>hoon</u>-toh

. . . save the attached file?   . . . *guardo el archivo adjunto?*
<u>gwar</u>-doh el ahr-<u>chee</u>-voh ad-<u>hoon</u>-toh

709. Just drag it and drop it. (inf.)   *Sólo arrástralo y colócalo.*
<u>Soh</u>-loh ah-<u>rahss</u>-trah-loh ee koh-<u>loh</u>-kah-loh

710.   Downloading software is risky.
       Descargar programas es riesgoso.
       Dess-kar-<u>gar</u> proh-<u>grah</u>-mahss ess ree-ess-<u>goh</u>-soh

711.   I think it doesn't have the software I need.
       Creo que no tiene el programa que necesito.
       <u>Kreh</u>-oh keh noh tee-<u>eh</u>-neh el proh-<u>grah</u>-mah keh
       neh-seh-<u>see</u>-toh

712.   Does this computer have antivirus software?
       ¿Tiene un programa antivirus esta computadora?
       Tee-<u>eh</u>-neh oon proh-<u>grah</u>-mah ahn-tee-<u>vee</u>-roos <u>ess</u>-tah
       kohm-poo-tah-<u>doh</u>-rah

713.   Did you remember to back up your work? (inf.)
       ¿Te acordaste de respaldar tu trabajo?
       Teh ah-kor-<u>dahss</u>-teh deh ress-pahl-<u>dahr</u> too trah-<u>bah</u>-hoh

714.   Don't forget to turn off the equipment. (inf.)
       No olvides apagar el equipo.
       Noh ohl-<u>vee</u>-dess ah-pah-<u>gar</u> el eh-<u>kee</u>-poh

BUSINESS TRAVEL

715.   I came for a conference.   *Vine a una conferencia.*
       <u>Vee</u>-neh ah <u>oo</u>-nah kohn-feh-<u>ren</u>-see-ah

       . . . a symposium.   . . . *un simposio.*   oon seem-<u>poh</u>-see-oh

       . . . a convention.   . . . *una convención.*
       <u>oo</u>-nah kohn-ven-see-<u>ohn</u>

       . . . a (professional) meeting.   . . . *una reunión (profesional).*
       <u>oo</u>-nah reh-oo-nee-<u>ohn</u> (proh-feh-see-oh-<u>nahl</u>)

       . . . an industry fair.   . . . *una feria industrial.*
       <u>oo</u>-nah <u>fehr</u>-ee-ah een-doos-tree-<u>ahl</u>

716.   I'm taking a (Spanish) course.
       Estoy tomando un curso (de español).
       Ess-<u>toy</u> toh-<u>mahn</u>-doh oon <u>koor</u>-soh (deh ess-pah-<u>nyohl</u>)

717.   I'm here on official business.
       Estoy aquí por asuntos oficiales.
       Ess-<u>toy</u> ah-<u>kee</u> por ahss-<u>soon</u>-tohss oh-fee-see-<u>ah</u>-less

718. I work for a transnational company.
Trabajo para una compañía transnacional.
Trah-<u>bah</u>-hoh pah-rah <u>oo</u>-nah kohm-pah <u>nyee</u>-ah
trahns-nah-see-oh-<u>nahl</u>

   ... an import/export business.
   ... una empresa de importación/exportación.
   <u>oo</u>-nah em-<u>preh</u>-sah deh eem-por-tah-see-<u>ohn</u>/ex-por-tah-see-<u>ohn</u>

719. I teach at a (state) university.
Enseño en una universidad (estatal).
En-<u>seh</u>-nyoh en <u>oo</u>-nah oo-nee-vehr-see-<u>dahd</u> (ess-tah-<u>tahl</u>)

720. I'm a government agent. *Soy un agente del gobierno.*
Soy oon ah-<u>hen</u>-teh del goh-bee-<u>ehr</u>-noh

721. We have offices all over the world.
Tenemos oficinas en todo el mundo.
Teh-<u>neh</u>-mohss oh-fee-<u>see</u>-nahss en <u>toh</u>-doh el <u>moon</u>-doh

722. The meeting is at eleven sharp.
La junta es a las once en punto.
Lah <u>hoon</u>-tah es ah lahss <u>ohn</u>-seh en <u>poon</u>-toh

723. I don't want to be late. *No quiero llegar tarde.*
Noh kee-<u>eh</u>-roh yeh-<u>gar</u> <u>tar</u>-deh

724. I'm late, forgive me. (for.) *Estoy retrasado, disculpe.*
Ess-<u>toy</u> reh-trah-<u>sah</u>-doh, dees-<u>kool</u>-peh

725. I have an appointment with the President.
Tengo una cita con el presidente.
<u>Ten</u>-goh <u>oo</u>-nah <u>see</u>-tah kohn el preh-see-<u>den</u>-teh

   ... the Vice-President (for Sales).
   ... el vicepresidente (de ventas).
   el vee-seh-preh-see-<u>den</u>-teh (deh <u>ven</u>-tahss)

726. I came to see the (Marketing) Director.
Vine a ver al director (de mercadeo).
<u>Vee</u>-neh ah vehr ahl dee-rek-<u>tor</u> (deh mehr-kah-<u>deh</u>-oh)

   ... the Assistant Director (for Human Resources).
   ... al subdirector (de recursos humanos).
   ahl soob-dee-rek-<u>tor</u> (deh reh-<u>koor</u>-sohss oo-<u>mah</u>-nohss)

727. I need to talk to the (Regional) Manager.
Necesito hablar con el gerente (regional).
Neh-seh-<u>see</u>-toh ah-<u>blar</u> kohn el heh-<u>ren</u>-teh (reh-hee-oh-<u>nahl</u>)

728. My name is . . .   *Mi nombre es . . .*   Mee <u>nohm</u>-breh ess . . .

729. Where is his/her office?   *¿Dónde está su oficina?*
<u>Dohn</u>-deh ess-<u>tah</u> soo oh-fee-<u>see</u>-nah

   . . . the elevator?   . . . *el elevador/ascensor?*
   el eh-leh-vah-<u>dor</u>/ah-sen-<u>sor</u>

730. I (don't) need an interpreter.   *(No) Necesito un intérprete.*
(Noh) Neh-seh-<u>see</u>-toh oon een-<u>tehr</u>-preh-teh

731. Do you have a business card? (for.)   *¿Tiene una tarjeta?*
Tee-<u>eh</u>-neh <u>oo</u>-nah tar-<u>heh</u>-tah

732. Here is my card.   *Aquí está mi tarjeta.*
Ah-<u>kee</u> ess-<u>tah</u> mee tar-<u>heh</u>-tah

733. I need to call headquarters.
Necesito llamar a la oficina central.
Neh-seh-<u>see</u>-toh yah-<u>mar</u> ah lah oh-fee-<u>see</u>-nah sen-<u>trahl</u>

   . . . my boss.   . . . *a mi jefe.*   ah mee <u>heh</u>-feh

   . . . my spouse.   . . . *a mi esposo/-a.*
   ah mee ess-<u>poh</u>-soh/-ah

734. Can we sign the contract now?
¿Podemos firmar el contrato ahora?
Poh-<u>deh</u>-mohss feer-<u>mar</u> el kohn-<u>trah</u>-toh ah-<u>oh</u>-rah

735. Some of the clauses aren't clear.
Algunas de las claúsulas no están claras.
Ahl-<u>goo</u>-nahss deh lahss <u>klow</u>-soo-lahss noh ess-<u>tahn</u>
<u>klah</u>-rahss

736. We need more time to think it over.
Necesitamos más tiempo para pensarlo.
Neh-seh-see-<u>tah</u>-mohss mahss tee-<u>em</u>-poh
<u>pah</u>-rah- pen-<u>sahr</u>-loh

737. I need to discuss it with my partners.
Necesito discutirlo con mis socios.
Neh-seh-<u>see</u>-toh dees-koo-<u>teer</u>-loh kohn mees <u>soh</u>-see-ohss

738.   The governing board has to approve it.
       La junta directiva tiene que aprobarlo.
       Lah <u>hoon</u>-tah dee-rek-<u>tee</u>-vah tee-<u>eh</u>-neh kch ah proh-<u>har</u>-loh

739.   The stockholders might not approve the deal.
       Los accionistas podrían no aprobar el trato.
       Lohss ahk-see-oh-<u>nees</u>-tahss poh-<u>dree</u>-ahn noh ah-proh-<u>bahr</u>
       el <u>trah</u>-toh

740.   We made an all-around excellent deal.
       Hicimos un negocio redondo.
       Ee-<u>see</u>-mohss oon neh-<u>goh</u>-see-oh reh-<u>dohn</u>-doh

741.   We're going to make a lot of money.
       Vamos a hacer mucho dinero.
       <u>Vah</u>-mohss ah ah-<u>sehr</u> <u>moo</u>-choh dee-<u>neh</u>-roh

742.   Let's go celebrate it.   *Vamos a celebrarlo.*
       <u>Vah</u>-mohss ah seh-leh-<u>brar</u>-loh

THE ENVIRONMENT

743.   I'm concerned about the environment.
       Me preocupa el medio ambiente.
       Meh preh-oh-<u>koo</u>-pah el <u>meh</u>-dee-oh ahm-bee-<u>en</u>-teh

       . . . global warming.   . . . *el calentamiento global.*
       el kahl-en-tah-mee-<u>en</u>-toh gloh-<u>bahl</u>

       . . . climate change.   . . . *los cambios climáticos.*
       lohss <u>kahm</u>-bee-ohss klee-<u>mah</u>-tee-kohss

       . . . melting ice caps.   . . . *el deshielo de los polos.*
       el dess-<u>yeh</u>-loh deh lohss <u>poh</u>-lohss

       . . . air/water pollution.   . . . *la contaminación del aire/agua.*
       lah kohn-tah-mee-nah-see-<u>ohn</u> del <u>I</u>-ray/ <u>ah</u>-wah

       . . . overpopulation.   . . . *la sobrepoblación.*
       lah soh-breh-poh-blah-see-<u>ohn</u>

744.   This city is very polluted.
       Esta ciudad está muy contaminada.
       <u>Ess</u>-tah <u>see</u>-oo-dahd ess-<u>tah</u> mooy kohn-tah-mee-<u>nah</u>-dah

745.   There is too much trash.   *Hay demasiada basura.*
       I deh-mah-see-<u>ah</u>-dah bah-<u>soo</u>-rah

746. It seems like there are too many cars.
Parece que hay demasiados autos.
Pah-<u>reh</u>-seh keh I deh-mah-see-<u>ah</u>-dohss <u>ow</u>-tohss

747. Why not use more bicycles?
¿Por qué no usar más bicicletas?
Por keh noh oo-<u>sar</u> mahss bee-see-<u>kleh</u>-tahss

748. People smoke too much.   *La gente fuma demasiado.*
Lah <u>hen</u>-teh <u>foo</u>-mah deh-mah-see-<u>ah</u>-doh

749. I never litter.   *Nunca tiro basura en la calle.*
<u>Noon</u>-kah <u>tee</u>-roh bah-<u>soo</u>-rah en lah <u>kah</u>-yeh

750. Where is there a recycling center?
¿Dónde hay un centro de reciclaje?
<u>Dohn</u>-deh I oon <u>sen</u>-troh deh reh-see-<u>klah</u>-heh

751. Do you recycle paper/cardboard?   *¿Reciclan papel/cartón?*
Reh-<u>see</u>-klahn pah-<u>pel</u>/kar-<u>tohn</u>

. . . plastics?   . . . *plásticos?*   <u>plahss</u>-tee-kohss

. . . glass?   . . . *vidrio?*   <u>vee</u>-dree-oh

. . . aluminum?   . . . *aluminio?*   ah-loo-<u>mee</u>-nee-oh

752. Let's not waste water/food.
No desperdiciemos agua/comida.
Noh dess-pehr-dee-see-<u>eh</u>-mohss <u>ah</u>-wah/koh-<u>mee</u>-dah

753. Let's turn off the lights.   *Apaguemos las luces.*
Ah-pah-<u>geh</u>-mohss lahss <u>loo</u>-sess

754. Let's turn down the air conditioning.
Bajemos el aire acondicionado.
Bah-<u>heh</u>-mohss el <u>I</u>-reh ah-kohn-dee-see-oh-<u>nah</u>-doh

755. We must care for nature.   *Debemos cuidar la naturaleza.*
Deh-<u>beh</u>-mohss kwee-<u>dar</u> lah nah-too-rah-<u>leh</u>-sah

756. The endangered species must be protected.
Hay que proteger las especies en peligro.
I keh proh-teh-<u>hehr</u> lahss ess-<u>peh</u>-see-ess en peh-<u>lee</u>-groh

757. I would like to visit a natural reserve.
Me gustaría visitar una reserva natural.
Meh goos-tah-<u>ree</u>-ah vee-see-tahr oo-nah reh <u>sehr</u>-vah
nah-too-<u>rahl</u>

758. It would be better if we planted our own food.
Sería mejor si plantáramos nuestra propia comida.
Seh-<u>ree</u>-ah meh-<u>hor</u> see plahn-<u>tar</u>-ah-mohss <u>nwess</u>-trah
<u>proh</u>-pree-ah koh-<u>mee</u>-dah

759. I want to buy organic products.
Quiero comprar productos orgánicos.
Kee-<u>eh</u>-roh kohm-<u>prar</u> proh-<u>dook</u>-tohss or-<u>gah</u>-nee-kohss

760. Where are local products sold?
¿Dónde se venden productos locales?
<u>Dohn</u>-deh seh <u>ven</u>-den proh-<u>dook</u>-tohss loh-<u>kah</u>-less

761. What is locally produced?   *¿Qué se produce localmente?*
Keh seh proh-<u>doo</u>-seh loh-kahl-<u>men</u>-teh

SPORTS & EXERCISE

762. I'm (not) in good shape.   *(No) Estoy en buena forma.*
(Noh) Ess-<u>toy</u> en <u>bweh</u>-nah <u>for</u>-mah

763. I (don't) like to exercise.   *(No) Me gusta hacer ejercicio.*
(Noh) Meh <u>goos</u>-tah ah-<u>sehr</u> eh-hehr-<u>see</u>-see-oh

764. It makes me feel good.   *Me hace sentir bien.*
Meh <u>ah</u>-seh sen-<u>teer</u> bee-<u>en</u>

765. I want to jog in the park.   *Quiero correr en el parque.*
Kee-<u>eh</u>-roh koh-<u>rehr</u> en el <u>par</u>-keh

766. Can I walk around here?   *¿Puedo caminar por aquí?*
<u>Pweh</u>-doh kah-mee-<u>nar</u> por ah-<u>kee</u>

767. I would like to go to the gym.   *Me gustaría ir al gimnasio.*
Meh goos-tah-<u>ree</u>-ah eer ahl heem-<u>nah</u>-see-oh

    . . . go swimming.   . . . *ir a nadar.*   eer ah nah-<u>dar</u>

    . . . ride a bike.   . . . *andar en bicicleta.*
ahn-<u>dar</u> en bee-see-<u>kleh</u>-tah

768. Do you like sports?   *¿Te gustan los deportes?*
Teh <u>goos</u>-tahn lohss deh-<u>por</u>-tess

769. What's your favorite sport?   *¿Cuál es tu deporte favorito?*
Kwahl ess too deh-<u>por</u>-teh fah-voh-<u>ree</u>-toh

770. Is there a national sport?   *¿Hay un deporte nacional?*
I oon deh-<u>por</u>-teh nah-see-oh-<u>nahl</u>

771. I prefer watching sports on TV.
Prefiero ver los deportes en la televisión.
Preh-fee-<u>eh</u>-roh vehr lohss deh-<u>por</u>-tess en lah
teh-leh-vee-see-<u>ohn</u>

772. I lift weights.   *Levanto pesas.*   Leh-<u>vahn</u>-toh <u>peh</u>-sahss

773. I practice martial arts.   *Practico artes marciales.*
Prahk-<u>tee</u>-koh <u>ahr</u>-tess mar-see-<u>ah</u>-less

774. Have you tried yoga? (inf.)   *Has probado el yoga?*
Ahss proh-<u>bah</u>-doh el <u>yoh</u>-gah?

775. I do aerobics.   *Hago ejercicios aeróbicos.*
<u>Ah</u>-goh eh-hehr-<u>see</u>-see-ohss I-<u>roh</u>-bee-kohss

776. I train every day.   *Me entreno todos los días*
Meh en-<u>treh</u>-noh <u>toh</u>-dohss lohss <u>dee</u>-ahss

777. I really like playing golf.   *Me encanta jugar golf.*
Meh en-<u>kahn</u>-tah hoo-<u>gar</u> gohlf
. . . tennis.   . . . *tenis.*   <u>teh</u>-nees
. . . basketball.   . . . *baloncesto.*   bah-lohn-<u>sess</u>-toh
. . . volleyball.   . . . *voleibol.*   voh-lay-<u>bohl</u>

778. Can we go to a soccer match?
¿Podemos ir a un partido de futbol?
Poh-<u>deh</u>-mohss eer ah oon par-<u>tee</u>-doh deh <u>foot</u>-bohl

779. What's the local team's name?
¿Cómo se llama el equipo local?
<u>Koh</u>-moh seh <u>yah</u>-mah el eh-<u>kee</u>-poh loh-<u>kahl</u>

780. Are they good?   *¿Son buenos?*   Sohn <u>bweh</u>-nohss

781. Are you a (big) fan? (inf.)   ¿*Eres un (gran) hincha?*
Eh-ress oon (grahn) <u>een</u>-chah

782. When is the bull-fighting season?
¿*Cuándo es la temporada de toros?*
<u>Kwahn</u>-doh ess lah tem-poh-<u>rah</u>-dah deh <u>toh</u>-rohss

783. Is boxing/wrestling popular?
¿*Es popular el boxeo/la lucha libre?*
Ess poh-poo-<u>lar</u> el bohk-<u>seh</u>-oh/lah <u>loo</u>-chah <u>lee</u>-breh

HEALTH & WELLNESS

784. I don't feel well.   *No me siento bien.*
Noh meh see-<u>en</u>-toh bee-<u>en</u>

785. I feel (very) ill.   *Me siento (muy) mal.*
Meh see-<u>en</u>-toh (mooy) mahl

786. I've been feeling sick since yesterday.
Me siento mal desde ayer.
Meh see-<u>en</u>-toh mahl <u>dess</u>-deh ah-<u>yehr</u>

   . . . since two days ago.   . . . *desde hace dos días.*
   <u>dess</u>-deh <u>ah</u>-seh dohss <u>dee</u>-ahss

   . . . since a week ago.   . . . *desde hace una semana.*
   <u>dess</u>-deh <u>ah</u>-seh <u>oo</u>-nah seh-<u>mah</u>-nah

   . . . since I got here.   . . . *desde que llegué.*
   <u>dess</u>-deh keh yeh-<u>geh</u>

787. I'm (very) sick.   *Estoy (muy) enfermo/-a.*
Ess-<u>toy</u> (mooy) en-<u>fehr</u>-moh/-ah

788. I need a doctor (who speaks English).
Necesito un médico/doctor (que hable inglés).
Neh-seh-<u>see</u>-toh oon <u>meh</u>-dee-koh/dohk-<u>tor</u> keh <u>ah</u>-bleh
een-<u>gless</u>

   . . . a general practitioner.   . . . *un médico generalista.*
   oon <u>meh</u>-dee-koh heh-nehr-ah-<u>lees</u>-tah

   . . . a specialist.   . . . *un especialista.*
   oon ess-peh-see-ahl-<u>ees</u>-tah

   . . . a dentist.   . . . *un dentista.*   oon den-<u>tees</u>-tah

789. Where can I get a medical examination?
¿Dónde puedo obtener una consulta médica?
Dohn-deh **pweh**-doh ohb-teh-**nehr** **oo**-nah kohn-**sool**-tah **meh**-dee-kah

790. I would rather see a female doctor.
Preferiría ver a una doctora.
Preh-feh-ree-**ree**-ah vehr ah **oo**-nah dohk-**tor**-ah

791. Can a doctor come here?   *¿Puede venir un doctor aquí?*
Pweh-deh ven-**eer** oon dohk-**tor** ah-**kee**

792. Call an ambulance.   *Llamen una ambulancia.*
Yah-men **oo**-nah ahm-boo-**lahn**-see-ah

793. I want to go to the hospital.   *Quiero ir al hospital.*
Kee-**eh**-roh eer ahl ohss-pee-**tahl**
. . . to the clinic.   . . . *a la clínica.*   ah lah **klee**-nee-kah
. . . to the Emergency Room.
. . . *a la sala de emergencias/urgencias. (Mex.)*
ah lah **sah**-lah deh eh-mehr-**hen**-see-ahss/oor-**hen**-see-ahss

794. Do I need to make an appointment?   *¿Debo hacer una cita?*
Deh-boh ah-**sehr** **oo**-nah **see**-tah

795. It's an emergency.   *Es una emergencia.*
Ess **oo**-nah eh-mehr-**hen**-see-ah

796. It's urgent.   *Es urgente.*   Ess oor-**hen**-teh

797. I'm about to give birth.   *Estoy a punto de dar a luz.*
Ess-**toy** ah **poon**-toh deh dahr ah loos

798. I'm dying.   *Me muero.*   Meh **mweh**-roh

799. I have a (high) fever/a (high) temperature.
Tengo (mucha) fiebre/una temperatura (alta).
Ten-goh (**moo**-chah) fee-**eh**-breh/**oo**-nah tem-peh-rah-**too**-rah (**ahl**-tah)

800. I feel a (sharp) pain here.   *Siento un (fuerte) dolor aquí.*
See-**en**-toh oon (**fwehr**-teh) doh-**lor** ah-**kee**

801. [My head] hurts (a lot).   *Me duele (mucho) la cabeza.*
Meh <u>dweh</u>-leh (<u>moo</u>-choh) lah kah-<u>beh</u>-sah

My (inner) ear . . .   . . . *el oído.*   el oh-<u>ee</u>-doh

My tooth . . .   . . . *el diente.*   el dee-<u>en</u>-teh

My neck . . .   . . . *el cuello.*   el <u>kweh</u>-yoh

My throat . . .   . . . *la garganta.*   lah gar-<u>gahn</u>-tah

My shoulder . . .   . . . *el hombro.*   el <u>ohm</u>-broh

My back . . .   . . . *la espalda.*   lah ess-<u>pahl</u>-dah

My chest . . .   . . . *el pecho.*   el <u>peh</u>-choh

My left/right arm . . .   . . . *el brazo izquierdo/derecho.*
el <u>brah</u>-soh ees-kee-<u>ehr</u>-doh/deh-<u>reh</u>-choh

My elbow . . .   . . . *el codo.*   el <u>koh</u>-doh

My wrist . . .   . . . *la muñeca.*   lah moo-<u>nyeh</u>-kah

My hand . . .   . . . *la mano.*   lah <u>mah</u>-noh

My finger . . .   . . . *el dedo.*   el <u>deh</u>-doh

My waist . . .   . . . *la cintura.*   lah seen-<u>too</u>-rah

My stomach . . .   . . . *el estomago.*   el ess-<u>toh</u>-mah-goh

My hip . . .   . . . *la cadera.*   lah kah-<u>deh</u>-rah

My leg . . .   . . . *la pierna.*   lah pee-<u>ehr</u>-nah

My knee . . .   . . . *la rodilla.*   lah roh-<u>dee</u>-yah

My ankle . . .   . . . *el tobillo.*   el toh-<u>bee</u>-yoh

My foot . . .   . . . *el pie.*   el pee-<u>eh</u>

My toe . . .   . . . *el dedo del pie.*   el <u>deh</u>-doh del pee-<u>eh</u>

802. I'm dizzy.   *Estoy mareado/-a.*   Ess-<u>toy</u> mar-eh-<u>ah</u>-doh/-ah

. . . constipated.   . . . *constipado/-a/estreñido/-a.*
kohn-stee-<u>pah</u>-doh/-ah/ess-treh-<u>nyee</u>-doh/-ah

. . . swollen.   . . . *hinchado/-a.*   een-<u>chah</u>-doh/-ah

. . . pregnant.   . . . *embarazada.*   em-bah-rah-<u>sah</u>-dah

. . . bleeding (a lot).   . . . *sangrando (mucho).*
sahn-<u>grahn</u>-doh (<u>moo</u>-choh)

803. It itches (a lot).   *Siento (mucha) comezón.*
See-<u>en</u>-toh (<u>moo</u>-chah) koh-<u>meh</u>-<u>sohn</u>

804. I feel nauseous.   *Siento náuseas.*   See-<u>en</u>-toh <u>now</u>-seh-ahss

805. I suffer from indigestion.   *Sufro de indigestión.*
      <u>Soo</u>-froh deh een-dee-gess-tee-<u>ohn</u>

      . . . heartburn.   *agruras/acidez estomacal.*
      ah-<u>groo</u>-rahss/ah-<u>see</u>-dess ess-toh-mah-<u>kahl</u>

806. . . . (chronic) sinusitis.   . . . *sinusitis (crónica).*
      see-noo-<u>see</u>-tees (<u>kroh</u>-nee-kah)

807. I can't breathe.   *No puedo respirar.*
      Noh <u>pweh</u>-doh ress-pee-<u>rar</u>

      . . . see (clearly).   . . . *ver (claramente).*
      vehr (klah-rah-<u>men</u>-teh)

      . . . hear (well).   . . . *oír (bien).*   oh-<u>eer</u> (bee-<u>en</u>)

      . . . sleep.   . . . *dormir.*   dor-<u>meer</u>

      . . . move my arm/my legs.   . . . *mover el brazo/las piernas.*
      moh-<u>vehr</u> el <u>brah</u>-soh/lahss pee-<u>ehr</u>-nahss

      . . . speak.   . . . *hablar.*   ah-<u>blar</u>

808. Something I ate made me ill.   *Algo que comí me hizo daño.*
      <u>Ahl</u>-goh keh koh-<u>mee</u> meh <u>ee</u>-soh <u>dah</u>-nyoh

809. I threw up (a lot).   *Vomité (mucho).*
      Voh-mee-<u>teh</u> (<u>moo</u>-choh)

810. I can't stop throwing up.   *No puedo dejar de vomitar.*
      Noh <u>pweh</u>-doh deh-<u>har</u> deh voh-mee-<u>tar</u>

811. Something bit me. (an insect)   *Algo me picó.*
      <u>Ahl</u>-goh meh pee-<u>koh</u>

812. Something bit me. (an animal)   *Algo me mordió.*
      <u>Ahl</u>-goh meh mor-dee-<u>oh</u>

813. I hurt myself.   *Me lastimé.*   Meh lahss-tee-<u>meh</u>

814. I hurt my hand/my foot.   *Me lastimé la mano/el pie.*
      Meh lahss-tee-<u>meh</u> lah <u>mah</u>-noh/el pee-<u>eh</u>

815. I twisted my wrist/my ankle.   *Me torcí la muñeca/el tobillo.*
      Meh tor-<u>see</u> lah moo-<u>nyeh</u>-kah/el toh-<u>bee</u>-yoh

816. I broke my arm/my leg.   *Me rompí el brazo/la pierna.*
      Meh rohm-<u>pee</u> el <u>brah</u>-soh/lah pee-<u>ehr</u>-nah

817. I cut myself.   *Me corté.*   Meh kor-<u>teh</u>

818.   I may need some stitches.
       Puede que necesite unos puntos (de sutura).
       <u>Pweh</u>-deh keh neh-seh-<u>see</u>-teh oo-nohss <u>poon</u>-tohss
       (deh soo-<u>too</u>-rah)

819.   I burned myself.   *Me quemé.*   Meh keh-<u>meh</u>

820.   I have asthma.   *Tengo asma.*   <u>Ten</u>-goh <u>ahss</u>-mah
       . . . muscle cramps.   . . . *calambres musculares.*
       kah-<u>lahm</u>-bress moos-koo-<u>lah</u>-ress
       . . . cancer.   . . . *cáncer.*   <u>kahn</u>-sehr
       . . . diabetes.   . . . *diabetes.*   dee-ah-<u>beh</u>-tess
       . . . diarrhea.   . . . *diarrea.*   dee-ar-<u>reh</u>-ah
       . . . menstrual cramps.   . . . *dolores menstruales.*
       doh-<u>loh</u>-ress mens-<u>trwah</u>-less
       . . . chills.   . . . *escalofríos.*   ess-kah-loh-<u>free</u>-ohss
       . . . an S.T.D.   . . . *una enfermedad venérea/sexual.*
       <u>oo</u>-nah en-fehr-meh-<u>dahd</u> veh-<u>neh</u>-reh-ah/sek-soo-<u>ahl</u>
       . . . high/low blood pressure.   . . . *la presión alta/baja.*
       lah preh-see-<u>ohn</u> <u>ahl</u>-tah/<u>bah</u>-hah
       . . . hepatitis.   . . . *hepatitis.*   eh-pah-<u>tee</u>-tees
       . . . AIDS.   . . . *SIDA.*   <u>see</u>-dah
       . . . a cough.   . . . *tos.*   tohss

821.   I think I have an ear infection.
       Creo que tengo una infección del oído.
       <u>Kreh</u>-oh keh <u>ten</u>-goh <u>oo</u>-nah een-fek-see-<u>ohn</u> del oh-<u>ee</u>-doh
       . . . a skin infection.   . . . *infección de la piel.*
       een-fek-see-<u>ohn</u> deh lah pee-<u>el</u>
       . . . a urinary tract infection.   . . . *infección urinaria.*
       een-fek-see-<u>ohn</u> oo-ree-<u>nah</u>-ree-ah
       . . . a yeast infection.   . . . *infección vaginal.*
       een-fek-see-<u>ohn</u> vah-hee-<u>nahl</u>
       . . . a bladder infection.   . . . *infección de la vejiga.*
       een-fek-see-<u>ohn</u> deh lah veh-<u>hee</u>-gah

822.   I've had heart problems.   *He tenido problemas del corazón.*
       Eh teh-<u>nee</u>-doh proh-<u>bleh</u>-mahss del koh-rah-<u>sohn</u>

   . . . liver problems.   . . . *problemas del hígado.*
proh-<u>bleh</u>-mahss del <u>ee</u>-gah-doh

   . . . kidney problems.   . . . *problemas renales.*
proh-<u>bleh</u>-mahss reh-<u>nah</u>-less

   . . . lung problems.   . . . *problemas respiratorios.*
proh-<u>bleh</u>-mahss res-pee-rah-<u>toh</u>-ree-ohss

823. I'm allergic to penicillin.   *Soy alérgico a la penicilina.*
Soy ah-<u>lehr</u>-hee-koh ah lah peh-nee-see-<u>lee</u>-nah

   . . . to shellfish.   . . . *a los mariscos.*
ah lohss mah-<u>rees</u>-kohss

   . . . to peanuts.   . . . *a los cacahuates/al maní.*
ah lohss kah-kah-<u>wah</u>-tess/ahl mah-<u>nee</u>

   . . . to pollen.   . . . *al polen.*   **ahl <u>poh</u>-len**

   . . . to bee stings.   . . . *a las picaduras de abeja.*
ah lahss pee-kah-<u>doo</u>-rahss deh ah-<u>beh</u>-hah

824. I have hay fever.   *Tengo fiebre del heno.*
<u>Ten</u>-goh fee-<u>eh</u>-breh del <u>eh</u>-noh

825. My doctor prescribed this medicine.
Mi doctor me recetó esta medicina.
Mee dohk-<u>tor</u> meh reh-seh-<u>toh</u> ess-tah meh-dee-<u>see</u>-nah

826. I am taking pain-killers.   *Estoy tomando analgésicos.*
Ess-<u>toy</u> toh-<u>mahn</u>-doh ah-nahl-<u>heh</u>-see-kohss

   . . . antibiotics.   . . . *antibióticos.*
ahn-tee-bee-<u>oh</u>-tee-kohss

   . . . antihistamines.   . . . *antiestamínicos.*
ahn-tee-ess-tah-<u>mee</u>-nee-kohss

   . . . aspirin.   . . . *aspirinas.*   **ahss-pee-<u>ree</u>-nahss**

   . . . contraceptive pills.
   . . . *píldoras/pastillas anticonceptivas.*
<u>peel</u>-doh-rahss/pahss-<u>tee</u>-yahss ahn-tee-kohn-sep-<u>tee</u>-vahss

   . . . vitamins.   . . . *vitaminas.*   **vee-tah-<u>mee</u>-nahss**

827. I (don't) smoke.   *(No) Fumo.*   **(Noh) <u>Foo</u>-moh**

828. I (don't) drink alcohol.   *(No) Bebo alcohol.*
(Noh) <u>Beh</u>-boh ahl-<u>kohl</u>

829. I (don't) use drugs.   *(No) Uso drogas.*
      (Noh) <u>Oo</u>-soh <u>droh</u>-gahss

830. I wear contact lenses.   *Uso lentes de contacto.*
      <u>Oo</u>-soh <u>len</u>-tess deh kohn-<u>tahk</u>-toh

831. My blood type is O positive/negative.
      Mi tipo de sangre es O positivo/negativo.
      Mee <u>tee</u>-poh deh <u>sahn</u>-greh ess oh poh-see-<u>tee</u>-voh/
      neh-gah-<u>tee</u>-voh

832. Is it (very) serious?   *¿Es (muy) grave?*
      Ess (mooy) <u>grah</u>-veh

833. Will I be well (soon)?   *¿Estaré bien (pronto)?*
      Ess-tah-<u>reh</u> bee-<u>en</u> (<u>prohn</u>-toh)

834. How much for the visit?   *¿Cuánto es por la consulta?*
      <u>Kwahn</u>-toh ess por lah kohn-<u>sool</u>-tah

835. Where does one pay for the visit?
      ¿Dónde se paga la consulta?
      <u>Dohn</u>-deh seh <u>pah</u>-gah lah kohn-<u>sool</u>-tah

836. I need a receipt for my insurance company.
      Necesito un recibo para mi compañía de seguros.
      Neh-seh-<u>see</u>-toh oon reh-<u>see</u>-boh <u>pah</u>-rah mee
      kohm-pah-<u>nyee</u>-ah deh seh-<u>goo</u>-rohss

837. Can you give me something for the pain? (for.)
      ¿Me puede dar algo para el dolor?
      Meh <u>pweh</u>-deh dar <u>ahl</u>-goh <u>pah</u>-rah el doh-<u>lor</u>

838. I need medicine.   *Necesito medicina.*
      Neh-seh-<u>see</u>-toh meh-dee-<u>see</u>-nah

      . . . a Band-Aid.   *. . . una curita/tirita. (Sp.)*
      <u>oo</u>-nah koo-<u>ree</u>-tah/tee-<u>ree</u>-tah

      . . . a laxative.   *. . . un laxante.*   oon lahk-<u>sahn</u>-teh
      . . . a prescription.   *. . . una receta médica.*
      <u>oo</u>-nah reh-<u>seh</u>-tah <u>meh</u>-dee-kah

      . . . a tetanus shot.   *. . . una vacuna contra el tétano.*
      <u>oo</u>-nah vah-<u>koo</u>-nah <u>kohn</u>-trah el <u>teh</u>-tah-noh

      . . . a bandage.   *. . . una venda.*   <u>oo</u>-nah <u>ven</u>-dah

839. I don't want to have surgery here.
No quiero que me operen aquí.
Noh kee-<u>eh</u>-roh keh meh oh-<u>peh</u>-ren ah-<u>kee</u>

840. I hate needles.   *Odio las agujas.*
<u>Oh</u>-dee-oh lahss ah-<u>goo</u>-hahss

841. Seeing blood makes me sick.   *Me enferma ver sangre.*
Meh en-<u>fehr</u>-mah vehr <u>sahn</u>-greh

842. Where is the drugstore?   *¿Dónde está la farmacia?*
<u>Dohn</u>-deh ess-<u>tah</u> lah far-<u>mah</u>-see-ah

843. Is it open twenty-four hours?
¿Está abierta las veinticuatro horas?
Ess-<u>tah</u> ah-bee-<u>ehr</u>-tah lahss vayn-tee-<u>kwah</u>-troh <u>oh</u>-rahss

844. Are you a pharmacist? (for.)   *¿Es usted farmacéutico/-a?*
Ess oos-<u>ted</u> fahr-mah-<u>seh</u>-oo-tee-koh/kah

845. How do you take this medicine?
¿Cómo se toma esta medicina?
<u>Koh</u>-moh seh <u>toh</u>-mah <u>ess</u>-tah meh-dee-<u>see</u>-nah

846. Does this medicine cause side effects?
¿Causa efectos secundarios este medicamento?
<u>Kow</u>-sah eh-<u>fek</u>-tohss seh-koon-<u>dah</u>-ree-ohss <u>ess</u>-teh
meh-dee-kah-<u>men</u>-toh

847. Are they serious?   *¿Son serios?*   Sohn <u>seh</u>-ree-ohss

848. What are they?   *¿Cuáles son?*   <u>Kwah</u>-less sohn

CAR TROUBLE

849. The car broke down.   *Se descompuso el auto/el coche.*
Seh dess-kohm-<u>poo</u>-soh el <u>ow</u>-toh/el <u>koh</u>-cheh

850. We had an accident.   *Tuvimos un accidente.*
Too-<u>vee</u>-mohss oon ahk-see-<u>den</u>-teh

851. We crashed (with another car).   *Chocamos (con otro auto).*
Cho-<u>kah</u>-mohss (kohn <u>oh</u>-troh <u>ow</u>-toh)

852. It won't start.   *No enciende.*   **Noh en-see-<u>en</u>-deh**

853. It makes a funny noise.   *Hace un ruido raro.*
     <u>Ah</u>-seh oon <u>rwee</u>-doh <u>rah</u>-roh

854. It doesn't shift gears (smoothly).   *No embraga (fácilmente).*
     Noh em-<u>brah</u>-gah (<u>fah</u>-seel-men-teh)

855. The headlights won't turn on.   *No prenden los faros.*
     Noh <u>pren</u>-den lohss <u>fah</u>-rohss

     The brake lights . . .   . . . *las luces de atrás.*
     lahss <u>loo</u>-sess deh ah-<u>trahss</u>

     The turn signals . . .   . . . *las intermitentes.*
     lahss een-tehr-mee-<u>ten</u>-tess

856. The windshield wipers aren't moving.
     Los limpiadores no se mueven.
     Lohss leem-pee-ah-<u>doh</u>-ress noh seh <u>mweh</u>-ven

857. It doesn't brake well.   *No frena bien.*
     Noh <u>freh</u>-nah bee-<u>en</u>

858. It doesn't accelerate.   *No acelera.*   **Noh ah-seh-<u>leh</u>-rah**

859. It accelerates by itself.   *Acelera sólo.*
     Ah-ceh-<u>leh</u>-rah <u>soh</u>-loh

860. The pedal gets stuck.   *El pedal se atora.*
     El peh-<u>dahl</u> seh ah-<u>toh</u>-rah

861. The steering doesn't work.   *No funciona la dirección.*
     Noh foon-see-<u>oh</u>-nah lah dee-rek-see-<u>ohn</u>

862. It's blowing a lot of smoke.   *Echa mucho humo.*
     <u>Eh</u>-chah <u>moo</u>-choh <u>oo</u>-moh

863. It has a flat tire.   *Tiene una rueda pinchada.*
     Tee-<u>eh</u>-neh <u>oo</u>-nah <u>rweh</u>-dah peen-<u>chah</u>-dah

864. A tire went flat.   *Se le ponchó una llanta. (Mex.)*
     <u>Seh</u> leh pohn-<u>choh</u> <u>oo</u>-nah <u>yahn</u>-tah

865.   I think it has a dead battery.
       Creo que tiene la batería descargada.
       <u>Kreh</u>-oh keh tee-<u>eh</u>-neh lah bah-teh-<u>ree</u>-ah dess-kar-<u>gah</u>-dah

866.   It could be a blown gasket.   *Podría ser una junta reventada.*
       Poh-<u>dree</u>-ah sehr <u>oo</u>-nah <u>hoon</u>-tah reh-ven-<u>tah</u>-dah

867.   It's overheated.   *Está sobrecalentado.*
       Ess-<u>tah</u> <u>soh</u>-breh-kah-len-<u>tah</u>-doh

868.   It's leaking coolant.   *Está perdiendo anticongelante.*
       Ess-<u>tah</u> pehr-dee-<u>en</u>-doh ahn-tee-kohn-heh-<u>lahn</u>-teh

869.   It needs oil.   *Le falta aceite.*   Leh <u>fahl</u>-tah ah-<u>say</u>-teh
       . . . gas.   . . . *gasolina.*   gahss-soh-<u>lee</u>-nah
       . . . air in the tires.   . . . *aire a las llantas.*
       <u>I</u>-reh ah lahss <u>yahn</u>-tahss

870.   I left the keys inside.   *Dejé las llaves adentro.*
       Deh-<u>heh</u> lahss <u>yah</u>-vess ah-<u>den</u>-troh

871.   Where is there a car repair shop/garage?
       ¿Dónde hay un taller mecánico/un garaje?
       <u>Dohn</u>-deh I oon tah-<u>yehr</u> meh-<u>kah</u>-nee-koh/oon gah-<u>rah</u>-heh

872.   I need a tow truck.   *Necesito una grúa.*
       Neh-seh-<u>see</u>-toh <u>oo</u>-nah <u>groo</u>-ah
       . . . a (car) mechanic.   . . . *un mecánico (automotriz).*
       oon meh-<u>kah</u>-nee-koh (ow-toh-moh-<u>trees</u>)
       . . . a car jack.   . . . *un gato.*   oon <u>gah</u>-toh

873.   Do you have jumper cables?
       ¿Tiene cables/una pinza de batería? (Sp.)
       Tee-<u>eh</u>-neh <u>kah</u>-bless/<u>oo</u>-nah <u>peen</u>-sah deh bah-teh-<u>ree</u>-ah

874.   How much will it cost?   *¿Cuánto va a costar?*
       <u>Kwahn</u>-toh vah ah kohs-<u>tar</u>

875.   Does that include parts and labor?
       ¿Eso incluye mano de obra y refacciones?
       <u>Eh</u>-soh een-<u>kloo</u>-yeh <u>mah</u>-noh deh <u>oh</u>-brah ee
       reh-fahk-see-<u>oh</u>-ness

876.   Will you put in new parts? (for.)
        ¿Le pondrá refacciones nuevas?
        Leh pohn-<u>drah</u> reh-<u>falık-see-oh</u>-ness <u>nweh</u>-vahss

877.   Can you fix it (today)? (for.)
        ¿Puede arreglarlo/repararlo (hoy mismo)?
        Pweh-deh ah-reh-<u>glar</u>-loh/re-pah-<u>rar</u>-loh (oy <u>mees</u>-moh)

878.   When will it be ready?   *¿Cuándo estará listo?*
        <u>Kwahn</u>-doh ess-tah-<u>rah</u> <u>lees</u>-toh

879.   At what time can I pick it up?
        ¿A qué hora puedo recogerlo?
        Ah keh <u>oh</u>-rah <u>pweh</u>-doh reh-koh-<u>hehr</u>-loh

880.   It's (not) insured.   *(No) Está asegurado.*
        (Noh) Ess-<u>tah</u> ah-seh-goo-<u>rah</u>-doh

881.   Can I pay with a credit card?
        ¿Puedo pagar con tarjeta de crédito?
        <u>Pweh</u>-doh pah-<u>gar</u> kohn tar-<u>heh</u>-tah deh <u>kreh</u>-dee-toh

EMERGENCIES

882.   Help!   *¡Ayuda!/¡Auxilio!/¡Socorro!*
        Ah-<u>yoo</u>-dah/Owk-<u>see</u>-lee-oh/Soh-<u>koh</u>-roh

883.   Do you know first aid?   *¿Sabe primeros auxilios?*
        <u>Sah</u>-beh pree-<u>meh</u>-rohss owk-<u>see</u>-lee-ohss

884.   I need a doctor.   *Necesito un médico/un doctor.*
        Neh-seh-<u>see</u>-toh oon <u>meh</u>-dee-koh/oon dohk-<u>tor</u>

885.   Where is the nearest hospital?
        ¿Dónde está el hospital más cercano?
        <u>Dohn</u>-deh ess-<u>tah</u> el ohss-pee-<u>tahl</u> mahss sehr-<u>kah</u>-noh

886.   Take me to the Emergency Room.
        Lléveme a la sala de emergencias/urgencias. (Mex.)
        <u>Yeh</u>-veh-meh ah lah <u>sah</u>-lah deh eh-mehr-<u>hen</u>-see-ahss/
        oor-<u>hen</u>-see-ahss

887.   I'm going to pass out.   *Me voy a desmayar.*
        Meh voy ah dess-mah-<u>yahr</u>

888. I want a lawyer.   *Quiero un abogado.*
Kee-<u>eh</u>-roh oon ah-boh-<u>gah</u>-doh

889. Call the police. (pl.)   *Llamen a la policía.*
<u>Yah</u>-men ah lah poh-lee-<u>see</u>-ah

. . . an ambulance.   . . . *una ambulancia.*
<u>oo</u>-nah ahm-boo-<u>lahn</u>-see-ah

. . . the fire department.   . . . *a los bomberos.*
ah lohss bohm-<u>beh</u>-rohss

890. It's an emergency!   *¡Es una emergencia!*
Ess <u>oo</u>-nah eh-mehr-<u>hen</u>-see-ah

891. Do something, please. (for.)   *Haga algo, por favor.*
<u>Ah</u>-gah <u>ahl</u>-goh por fah-<u>vor</u>

892. Stop, thief!   *¡Alto, ladrón!*   <u>Ahl</u>-toh, lah-<u>drohn</u>

893. He went that way.   *Se fue por allá.*   Seh fweh por ah-<u>yah</u>

894. I have been robbed/assaulted.   *Me han robado/asaltado.*
Meh ahn roh-<u>bah</u>-doh/ah-sahl-<u>tah</u>-doh

895. They stole my wallet.   *Me robaron la cartera/la billetera.*
Meh roh-<u>bah</u>-ron lah kar-<u>teh</u>-rah/lah bee-yeh-<u>teh</u>-rah

896. They took my purse.
Se llevaron mi bolsa (Mex.)/mi bolso. (Sp.)
Seh yeh-<u>vah</u>-rohn mee <u>bohl</u>-sah/mee <u>bohl</u>-soh

. . . my luggage.   . . . *mi equipaje.*   mee eh-kee-<u>pah</u>-heh

897. I was raped.   *Me violaron.*   Meh vee-oh-<u>lah</u>-ron

898. I need to report a crime.   *Necesito hacer una denuncia.*
Neh-seh-<u>see</u>-toh ah-<u>sehr</u> <u>oo</u>-nah deh-<u>noon</u>-see-ah

899. I lost my passport.   *Perdí mi pasaporte.*
Pehr-<u>dee</u> mee pah-sah-<u>por</u>-teh

. . . my money.   . . . *mi dinero.*   mee dee-<u>neh</u>-roh

. . . my ticket.   . . . *mi boleto/pasaje.*
mee boh-<u>leh</u>-toh/pah-<u>sah</u>-heh

900. I can't find the key to my room.
No encuentro la llave de mi habitación.
Noh en-<u>kwen</u>-troh lah <u>yah</u>-veh deh mee ah-bee-tah-see-<u>ohn</u>

901. He/she can't swim.   *No sabe nadar.*   Noh <u>sah</u>-beh nah-<u>dar</u>

902. He/she's drowning.   *Se está ahogando,*
     Seh ess-<u>tah</u> ah-oh-<u>gahn</u>-doh

903. I think he/she's dead.   *Creo que está muerto/a.*
     <u>Kreh</u>-oh keh ess-<u>tah</u> <u>mwehr</u>-toh/-tah

FLIRTING

904. Hi, what's your name? (inf.)   *Hola, ¿cómo te llamas?*
     <u>Oh</u>-lah, <u>koh</u>-moh teh <u>yah</u>-mahss

905. My name is . . .   *Mi nombre es . . .*
     Mee <u>nohm</u>-breh ess . . .

906. I'm here on vacation.   *Estoy aquí de vacaciones.*
     Ess-<u>toy</u> ah-<u>kee</u> deh vah-kah-see-<u>oh</u>-ness

907. I came on business.   *Vine por negocios.*
     <u>Vee</u>-neh por neh-<u>goh</u>-see-ohss

908. I'm staying for the whole summer.
     Me quedo por todo el verano.
     Meh <u>keh</u>-doh por <u>toh</u>-doh el veh-<u>rah</u>-noh

     . . . for a week.   . . . *por una semana.*
     por <u>oo</u>-nah seh-<u>mah</u>-nah

     . . . for three days.   . . . *por tres días.*   por trehss <u>dee</u>-ahss

909. I'm leaving tomorrow.   *Me voy mañana.*
     Meh voy mah-<u>nyah</u>-nah

     . . . on Monday.   . . . *el lunes.*   el <u>loo</u>-ness

910. How old are you? (inf.)   *¿Cuántos años tienes?*
     <u>Kwahn</u>-tohss <u>ah</u>-nyohss tee-<u>en</u>-ess

911. I am (thirty) years old.   *Yo tengo (treinta) años.*
     Yoh <u>ten</u>-goh (<u>trayn</u>-tah) <u>ah</u>-nyohss

912. Do you work or do you study? (inf.)   *¿Estudias o trabajas?*
     Ess-<u>too</u>-dee-ahss oh trah-<u>bah</u>-hahss

913. What are you studying? (inf.)   *¿Qué estudias?*
      Keh ess-<u>too</u>-dee-ahss

914. Where do you work? (inf.)   *¿Dónde trabajas?*
      <u>Dohn</u>-deh trah-<u>bah</u>-hahss

915. Do you have a boyfriend/girlfriend? (inf.)
      ¿Tienes novio/-a?   **Tee-<u>eh</u>-ness <u>noh</u>-vee-oh/-ah**

916. Are you married? (inf.)   *¿Estás casado/-a?*
      Ess-<u>tahss</u> kah-<u>sah</u>-doh/-ah

917. How long have you been divorced? (inf.)
      ¿Hace cuánto tiempo que estás divorciado/-a?
      **<u>Ah</u>-seh <u>kwahn</u>-toh tee-<u>em</u>-poh keh ess-<u>tahss</u>
      dee-vor-see-<u>ah</u>-doh/-ah**

918. What music do you like? (inf.)   *¿Qué música te gusta?*
      Keh <u>moo</u>-see-kah teh <u>goos</u>-tah

919. Do you like movies? (inf.)   *¿Te gusta el cine?*
      Teh <u>goos</u>-tah el <u>see</u>-neh
      . . . literature?   . . . *la literatura?*   **lah lee-tehr-ah-<u>too</u>-rah**
      . . . poetry?   . . . *la poesía?*   **lah poh-eh-<u>see</u>-ah**
      . . . sports?   . . . *los deportes?*   **lohss deh-<u>por</u>-tehss**

920. What zodiac sign are you? (inf.)   *¿Qué signo eres?*
      Keh <u>seeg</u>-noh <u>eh</u>-ress

921. I'm a (Libra).   *Yo soy (Libra).*   **Yoh soy (<u>Lee</u>-brah)**

922. Don't bother me. (inf.)   *No me molestes.*
      Noh meh moh-<u>less</u>-tess

923. Leave me alone. (inf.)   *Déjame en paz.*
      <u>Deh</u>-hah-meh en pahss

924. I'm not interested.   *No estoy interesado/-a.*
      Noh ess-<u>toy</u> een-teh-reh-<u>sah</u>-doh/-ah

925. This guy is harassing me.   *Este tipo me está acosando.*
      <u>Ess</u>-teh <u>tee</u>-poh meh ess-<u>tah</u> ah-koh-<u>sahn</u>-doh

926. You're a (very) pretty girl. (inf.)
      Eres una chica (muy) bonita.
      Eh-ress **oo**-nah **chee**-kah (mooy) boh **nee**-tah

      . . . beautiful girl.   . . . *una chica bella/hermosa.*
      oo-nah **chee**-kah **beh**-yah/ehr-**moh**-sah

927. You're a (very) handsome man. (inf.)
      Eres un hombre (muy) guapo.
      Eh-ress oon **ohm**-breh (mooy) **wah**-poh

928. You have (very) pretty eyes. (inf.)
      Tienes unos ojos (muy) bonitos.
      Tee-**eh**-ness **oo**-nohss **oh**-hohss (mooy) boh-**nee**-tohss

      . . . a very beautiful smile.   . . . *una sonrisa preciosa.*
      oo-nah sohn-**ree**-sah preh-see-**oh**-sah

929. Do you want to go out with me? (inf.)
      ¿Quieres salir conmigo?   Kee-**eh**-ress sah-**leer** kohn-**mee**-goh

930. I want to go out with you. (inf.)   *Quiero salir contigo.*
      Kee-**eh**-roh sah-**leer** kohn-**tee**-goh

      . . . dance with you.   . . . *bailar contigo.*
      bi-**lar** kohn-**tee**-goh

      . . . talk with you.   . . . *hablar contigo.*
      ah-**blar** kohn-**tee**-goh

931. What are you doing tonight? (inf.)
      ¿Qué vas a hacer esta noche?
      Keh vahss ah ah-**sehr** **ess**-tah **noh**-cheh

932. Can we see each other tomorrow?
      ¿Nos podemos ver mañana?
      Nohss poh-**deh**-mohss vehr mah-**nyah**-nah

933. Have lunch/dinner with me. (inf.)
      Te invito a comer/cenar conmigo.
      Teh een-**vee**-toh ah koh-**mehr**/seh-**nar** kohn-**mee**-goh

934. Let me buy you a drink. (inf.)   *Deja que te invite una copa.*
      Deh-hah keh teh een-**vee**-teh **oo**-nah **koh**-pah

935. Come to the movies with me. *Acompáñame al cine.*
Ah-kohm-**pah**-nyah-meh ahl **see**-neh

936. Let's go (salsa) dancing. *Vamos a bailar (salsa).*
Vah-mohss ah bi-**lar** (**sahl**-sah)

937. (When) Can I call you? (inf.) *¿(Cuándo) Te puedo llamar?*
(**Kwahn**-doh) Teh **pweh**-doh yah-**mar**

938. I like you (a lot). [You're (very) nice.] (inf.)
Me caes (muy) bien. Meh **kah**-ess (mooy) bee-**en**

939. I like you (a lot). [I feel attracted to you.] (inf.)
Me gustas (mucho). Meh **goos**-tahss (**moo**-choh)

940. I love you. (inf.) *Te quiero.* Teh kee-**eh**-roh

941. I love you (heart and soul). [Seriously] (inf.)
Te amo (con toda el alma).
Teh **ah**-moh (kohn **toh**-dah el **ahl**-mah)

942. I want you. [Sexual] (inf.) *Te deseo.* Teh deh-**seh**-oh

943. Let me kiss you. (inf.) *Deja que te bese.*
Deh-hah keh teh **beh**-seh

944. Kiss me. (inf.) *Bésame.* **Beh**-sah-meh

945. Can I hold you in my arms? *¿Puedo abrazarte?*
Pweh-doh ah-brah-**sar**-teh

946. I want to make love to you. *Quiero hacerte el amor.*
Kee-**eh**-roh ah-**sehr**-teh el ah-**mor**

947. Not without a condom. *No sin un preservativo/condón.*
Noh seen oon preh-sehr-vah-**tee**-voh/kohn-**dohn**

948. Where can we get one? *¿Dónde podemos conseguir uno?*
Dohn-deh poh-**deh**-mohss kohn-seh-**geer** **oo**-noh

949. Thanks for a fun evening. *Gracias por una noche divertida.*
Grah-see-ahss por **oo**-nah **noh**-cheh dee-vehr-**tee**-dah

950. I had a wonderful evening. *Pase una noche maravillosa.*
Pah-**seh** **oo**-nah **noh**-cheh mah-rah-vee-**yoh**-sah

951. Will we see each other again?   *¿Nos volveremos a ver?*
Nohss vohl-vehr-<u>eh</u>-mohss ah vehr

952. I (don't) want to see you again.   *(No) Quiero volver a verte.*
(Noh) Kee-<u>eh</u>-roh vohl-<u>vehr</u> a <u>vehr</u>-teh

953. I will never forget you. (inf.)   *Nunca te olvidaré.*
<u>Noon</u>-kah teh ohl-vee-dah-<u>reh</u>

954. I will miss you (a lot). (inf.)   *Te extrañaré (mucho).*
Teh ex-trah-nyah-<u>reh</u> (<u>moo</u>-choh)

955. Don't leave me!   *¡No me dejes!*   Noh meh <u>deh</u>-hess

956. If you leave, don't come back.   *Si te vas, no regreses.*
See teh vahss noh reh-<u>greh</u>-sess

FAMILY, CHILDREN & PETS

957. I came with my girlfriend.   *Vine con mi novia.*
<u>Vee</u>-neh kohn mee <u>noh</u>-vee-ah

  . . . with my fiancée.   . . . *con mi prometida.*
kohn mee proh-meh-<u>tee</u>-dah

  . . . with my wife.   . . . *con mi esposa.*
kohn mee ess-<u>poh</u>-sah

958. I brought my family.   *Traje a mi familia.*
<u>Trah</u>-heh ah mee fah-<u>meel</u>-yah

  . . . my parents.   . . . *a mis padres.*   ah mees <u>pah</u>-dress
  . . . my in-laws.   . . . *a mis suegros.*   ah mees <u>sweh</u>-grohss

959. I'm here with my (favorite) aunt and uncle.
Estoy aquí con mis tíos (favoritos).
Ess-<u>toy</u> ah-<u>kee</u> kohn mees <u>tee</u>-ohss (fah-voh-<u>ree</u>-tohss)

960. How many brothers/sisters do you have?
¿Cuántos hermanos/as tienes?
<u>Kwahn</u>-tohss ehr-<u>mah</u>-nohss/ahss tee-<u>eh</u>-ness

961. I have one brother and one sister.
Tengo un hermano y una hermana.
<u>Ten</u>-goh oon ehr-<u>mah</u>-noh ee <u>oo</u>-nah ehr-<u>mah</u>-nah

962. This is my nephew/niece. *Este es mi sobrino/a.*
    Ess-teh ess mee soh-<u>bree</u>-noh/ah

    . . . my son/daughter. . . . *mi hijo/a.* mee <u>ee</u>-hoh/ah

    . . . my grandson/granddaughter. . . . *mi nieto/a.*
    mee nee-<u>eh</u>-toh/ah

963. These are my children. *Estos son mis hijos/as.*
    Ess-tohss sohn mees <u>ee</u>-hohss/ahss

964. How old are your children? (for./inf.)
    ¿Cuántos años tienen sus/tus hijos/as?
    <u>Kwahn</u>-tohss <u>ah</u>-nyohss tee-<u>eh</u>-nen soos/toos <u>ee</u>-hohss/ahss

965. They are three and five years old. *Tienen tres y cinco años.*
    Tee-<u>eh</u>-nen trehss ee <u>seen</u>-koh <u>ah</u>-nyohss

966. Where's your mom/dad? *¿Dónde está tu mamá/papá?*
    <u>Dohn</u>-deh ess-<u>tah</u> too mah-<u>mah</u>/pah-<u>pah</u>

967. Are there children's activities? *¿Hay actividades para niños?*
    I ahk-tee-vee-<u>dah</u>-dess <u>pah</u>-rah <u>nee</u>-nyohss

968. Where can we find a playground?
    ¿Dónde podemos encontrar un lugar de juegos/recreo?
    <u>Dohn</u>-deh poh-<u>deh</u>-mohss en-kohn-<u>trar</u> oon loo-<u>gar</u> de
    <u>hweh</u>-gohss/reh-<u>kreh</u>-oh

    . . . an amusement park? . . . *un parque de atracciones?*
    oon <u>par</u>-keh deh ah-trahk-see-<u>oh</u>-ness

    . . . a children's museum? . . . *un museo para niños?*
    oon moo-<u>seh</u>-oh <u>pah</u>-rah <u>nee</u>-nyohss

969. We're looking for a park with swings.
    Estamos buscando un parque con columpios.
    Ess-<u>tah</u>-mohss boos-<u>kahn</u>-doh oon <u>par</u>-keh kohn
    koh-<u>loom</u>-pee-ohss

970. Do you know of a children's show? (for.)
    ¿Sabe de un espectáculo para niños?
    <u>Sah</u>-beh deh oon ess-pek-<u>tah</u>-koo-loh <u>pah</u>-rah <u>nee</u>-nyohss

971.   Isn't there a kiddy pool somewhere?
       ¿No hay una alberca para niños en algún lado?
       Noh I <u>oo</u>-nah ahl-<u>behr</u>-kah <u>pah</u>-rah <u>nee</u>-nyohss en ahl-<u>goon</u>
       <u>lah</u>-doh

972.   Where can we find a toy store?
       ¿Dónde podemos encontrar una juguetería?
       <u>Dohn</u>-deh poh-<u>deh</u>-mohss en-kohn-<u>trar</u> <u>oo</u>-nah
       hoo-geh-teh-<u>ree</u>-ah

973.   We want to buy traditional toys.
       Queremos comprar juguetes tradicionales.
       Keh-<u>reh</u>-mohss kohm-<u>prar</u> hoo-<u>geh</u>-tess
       trah-dee-see-oh-<u>nah</u>-less

974.   Do you sell educational games?   *¿Venden juegos educativos?*
       <u>Ven</u>-den <u>hweh</u>-gohss eh-doo-kah-<u>tee</u>-vohss

975.   Do you have children's books?   *¿Tienen libros para niños?*
       Tee-<u>eh</u>-nen <u>lee</u>-brohss <u>pah</u>-rah <u>nee</u>-nyohss

976.   Can we go in the museum with the stroller?
       ¿Podemos entrar al museo con el cochecito/la carriola? (Mex.)
       Poh-<u>deh</u>-mohss en-<u>trar</u> ahl moo-<u>seh</u>-oh kohn el
       koh-cheh-<u>see</u>-toh/lah kah-ree-<u>oh</u>-lah

977.   We prefer a family-friendly restaurant.
       Preferimos un restaurante para familias.
       Preh-feh-<u>ree</u>-mohss oon res-tow-<u>rahn</u>-teh <u>pah</u>-rah
       fah-<u>meel</u>-yahss

978.   Do you have a children's menu?
       ¿Tienen un menú para niños?
       Tee-<u>eh</u>-nen oon meh-<u>noo</u> <u>pah</u>-rah <u>nee</u>-nyohss

979.   Can you bring us a high chair? (for.)
       ¿Nos puede traer una silla alta?
       Nohss <u>pweh</u>-deh trah-<u>ehr</u> <u>oo</u>-nah <u>see</u>-yah <u>ahl</u>-tah

980.   We need to see a pediatrician.
       Necesitamos ver a un pediatra.
       Neh-seh-see-<u>tah</u>-mohss vehr ah oon peh-dee-<u>ah</u>-trah

981. We brought our dog/cat. *Trajimos a nuestro perro/gato.*
Trah-<u>hee</u>-mohss ah <u>nwes</u>-troh <u>peh</u>-roh/<u>gah</u>-toh

982. He/she is like family. *Es como de la familia.*
Ess <u>koh</u>-moh deh lah fah-<u>meel</u>-yah

983. We never travel without him/her.
Nunca viajamos sin él/ella.
<u>Noon</u>-kah vee-ah-<u>hah</u>-mohss seen el/<u>eh</u>-yah

984. Does he/she have to be quarantined?
¿Tiene que estar en cuarentena?
Tee-<u>eh</u>-neh keh ess-<u>tar</u> en kwah-ren-<u>teh</u>-nah

985. For how long? *¿Por cuánto tiempo?*
Por <u>kwahn</u>-toh tee-<u>em</u>-poh

986. Do you have a pet? (for./inf.) *¿Tiene(s) una mascota?*
Tee-<u>eh</u>-neh(s) <u>oo</u>-nah mahss-<u>koh</u>-tah

987. Do you like animals? *¿Te gustan los animales?*
Teh <u>goos</u>-tahn lohss ah-nee-<u>mah</u>-less

988. Can we have pets in the room?
¿Podemos tener mascotas en la habitación?
Poh-<u>deh</u>-mohss teh-<u>nehr</u> mahss-<u>koh</u>-tahss en lah
ah-bee-tah-see-<u>ohn</u>

989. He/she is housebroken/trained. *Está entrenado/a.*
Ess-<u>tah</u> en-treh-<u>nah</u>-doh/ah

990. He/she has all her vaccines. *Tiene todas sus vacunas.*
Tee-<u>eh</u>-neh <u>toh</u>-dahss soos vah-<u>koo</u>-nahss

991. He/she is very clean. *Es muy limpio/a.*
Ess mooy <u>leem</u>-pee-oh/ah

992. He/she doesn't bite/bark. *No muerde/ladra.*
Noh <u>mwehr</u>-deh/<u>lah</u>-drah

993. He/she doesn't have fleas. *No tiene pulgas.*
Noh tee-<u>eh</u>-neh <u>pool</u>-gahss

994. I'm going to walk the dog.   *Voy a pasear al perro.*
      Voy ah pah-seh-<u>ar</u> ahl <u>peh</u>-roh

995. Where do they sell animal food?
      ¿Dónde se vende comida para animales?
      <u>Dohn</u>-deh seh <u>ven</u>-deh koh-<u>mee</u>-dah <u>pah</u>-rah ah-nee-<u>mah</u>-less

996. We have to take him/her to the vet.
      Tenemos que llevarlo/la al veterinario.
      **Teh-<u>neh</u>-mohss keh yeh-<u>var</u>-loh/lah ahl
      veh-teh-ree-<u>nah</u>-ree-oh**

997. Where is the animal hospital?
      ¿Dónde está el hospital para animales?
      <u>Dohn</u>-deh ess-<u>tah</u> el ohss-pee-<u>tahl</u> <u>pah</u>-rah ah-nee-<u>mah</u>-less

A LITTLE SLANG

998. What's up, dude?   *¿Qué onda, che? (Arg.)*
      Keh <u>ohn</u>-dah cheh

      What's up, dude?   *¿Qué cuentas, choche? (Per.)*
      Keh <u>kwen</u>-tahss <u>cho</u>-cheh

      What's up, dude?   *¿Qué hubo, güevón? (Col.)*
      Keh <u>oo</u>-boh weh-<u>vohn</u>

      What's up, dude?   *¿Qué onda, güey? (Mex.)*
      Keh <u>ohn</u>-dah way

      What's up, dude?   *¿Qué pasa, tío/-a? (Sp.)*
      Keh <u>pah</u>-sah <u>tee</u>-oh/-ah

999. How cool!   *¡Qué bacano! (Col.)*   **Keh bah-<u>kah</u>-noh**
      How cool!   *¡Qué chévere! (Ven.)*   **Keh <u>cheh</u>-veh-reh**
      How cool!   *¡Qué chido! (Mex.)*   **Keh <u>chee</u>-doh**

1000. This is cool!   *¡Esto está brutal! (Hon.)*
      <u>Ess</u>-toh ess-<u>tah</u> broo-<u>tahl</u>

      This is cool!   *¡Esto está macanudo! (Arg.)*
      <u>Ess</u>-toh ess-<u>tah</u> mah-kah-<u>noo</u>-doh

This is cool!   ¡Esto es pura vida! (CR.)
Ess-toh ess **poo**-rah **vee**-dah

This is cool!   ¡Esto mola! (Sp.)   **Ess**-toh **moh**-lah

1001. Don't be stupid!   ¡No seas boludo/-a! (Arg.)
Noh **seh**-ahss boh-**loo**-doh/-ah

Don't be stupid!   ¡No seas cojudo/-a! (Per.)
Noh **seh**-ahss koh-**hoo**-doh/-ah

Don't be stupid!   ¡No seas gilipollas! (Sp.)
Noh **seh**-ahss hee-lee-**poy**-ahss

Don't be stupid!   ¡No seas pendejo/-a! (Mex.)
Noh **seh**-ahss pen-**deh**-hoh/-ah

Spanish Grammar Primer

This section offers some vocabulary tips and the barest essentials of Spanish grammar. It is a helpful resource for a beginner and can serve as a quick reference for a more advanced speaker.

Abstract grammar can be very helpful, but the best way to integrate language rules will always be through frequent real-life use. Listen to as much Spanish as you can (music, movies, and television are good resources), communicate in Spanish as often as you can, using the words and phrases in this book, and soon you won't need to think about the grammar at all.

English and Spanish Cognates

Cognates are words that derive from a common ancestor language. Most words in Spanish and many words in English come from Latin or Greek. As a result, there are a lot of words in English that are cognates of words in Spanish; most are easily recognizable. Since changes are slight and predictable, you can quickly expand your vocabulary in Spanish by taking note of the following:

1. Some words are the same in both languages (except that their pronunciation may vary, see below): color, crisis, drama, error, general, horror, probable, tropical, . . .
2. Some words add an extra vowel to the English word: cliente, evidente, ignorante, importante, parte, artista, pianista, problema, programa, contacto, perfecto, líquido, . . . *

---

* Please don't make the error, often parodied in movies, of thinking that adding an "o" at the end of every word in a sentence makes it sound like Spanish; native Spanish speakers will likely consider it rude.

3. Many words ending in -ty in English end in **-tad** or **-dad** in Spanish: facul**tad**, liber**tad**, curiosi**dad**, socie**dad**, eterni**dad**, capaci**dad**, reali**dad**, clari**dad**, . . .

4. Many words ending in -y in English end in **-ía**, **-ia**, or **-io** (depending on gender, see below): compañ**ía**, geograf**ía**, histor**ia**, farmac**ia**, diccionar**io**, ordinar**io**, . . . *

5. Words that end in -tion in English generally end in **-ción** in Spanish: na**ción**, administra**ción**, ac**ción**, fric**ción**, sec**ción**, emo**ción**, combina**ción**, contribu**ción**, . . .

6. Words that end in -ous in English often end in **-oso** in Spanish: gener**oso**, fam**oso**, preci**oso**, delici**oso**, tedi**oso**, contagi**oso**, curi**oso**, escandal**oso**, religi**oso**, . . .

Gender, Number, and Agreement

In Spanish, most nouns are gendered: *silla* (chair) and *mesa* (table) are feminine while *escritorio* (desk) and *sombrero* (hat) are masculine. However, not all feminine nouns end in -a, nor do all masculine nouns end in -o: *carne* (meat), *flor* (flower), *canción* (song), and *mano* (hand) are feminine, while *sobre* (envelope), *calor* (heat), *camión* (bus), and *clima* (weather) are masculine. In some cases, the gender of a noun will depend on the object to which it applies: *cantante* (singer) can be either feminine or masculine. Likewise, *orden* (order) is feminine when it refers to the order issued by an authority and masculine when it refers to the order of things.

The best way to figure out whether a noun is masculine or feminine is to look at its corresponding definite (*the*) or indefinite (*a/an/some*) article:

	Definite (*the*)		Indefinite (*a/an/some*)	
	Masculine	Feminine	Masculine	Feminine
Singular	el	la	un	una
Plural	los	las	unos	unas

It is important to be aware of noun gender because in Spanish, articles and adjectives belonging to a noun must agree in gender with the noun.

---

* In a few cases, cognates don't have exactly the same meaning in Spanish as they do in English: *policía* means "police" in Spanish; policy should be translated as *política*.

Esa flor azul es muy bonita.*	*That blue flower is very pretty.*
María es **una** cantante muy talentosa.	*María is a very talented singer.*
Pedro es **un** cantante muy talentoso.	*Pedro is a very talented singer.*

Likewise, nouns, adjectives, and articles must agree in number. In Spanish, plurality is expressed by adding an **-s** to words that end in a vowel, and **-es** to nouns that end in a consonant:

Las flores azules son mis preferidas.	*Blue flowers are my favorite.*
Pedro y María son **unos** cantantes muy buenos.†	*Pedro and María are very good singers.*

Possessive Adjectives

In Spanish possession is generally indicated by a set of adjectives which must agree in gender and number with the noun they describe, the possessed object.

my	mi/mis
your	tu/tus
your (for.)	su/sus
his	
her	
our	nuestro/nuestra/nuestros/nuestras
your (pl.)	vuestro/vuestra/vuestros/vuestras (Sp.)
	su/sus (L. Am.)
their	su/sus

---

* Adjectives that end in -e or a consonant don't change on account of gender:
La casa verde   *The green house*   El sombrero verde   *The green hat*
† When there are both feminine and masculine individuals or objects in a group, masculine adjectives and articles are used.

Mi casa es su casa.	*My house is your house. (for).* *
Su pelo es rubio y sus ojos son verdes.	*His/her hair is blond and his/her eyes are green.* †
Tenemos **nuestro** dinero y nuestras maletas.‡	We have our money and our suitcases.
Pedro y Juan están listos para su viaje.	*Pedro and Juan are ready for their trip.*

Diminutives

Diminutives are widely used in Spanish, particularly in Latin American Spanish. A diminutive can signify that something is smaller, but it can also serve to express endearment, to intensify an idea, or as a rhetorical device that "softens" and embellishes whatever is being said. Diminutives are particles that attach at the end of words either after the final consonant or by replacing the final vowel. There are a number of diminutive suffixes in Spanish, but the most common is **-ito(s)/-ita(s)**.

Sólo quiero un pedac**ito** muy pequeñ**ito** de pastel.
I only want a tiny little piece of cake.

Me llamo Juan, pero mis amigos me llaman Juan**ito**.
My name is John, but my friends call me Johnny.

Vivo en una cas**ita** muy linda con mis hij**itas** y mis perr**itos**.
I live in a very cute little house with my dear little daughters and my doggies.

---

* On formal address see the PRONOUNS section beginning on p. 105.

† In Spanish the gender of the possessor is not expressed by the possessive adjective. Gender information would be supplied by context or through an alternative structure such as: El pelo de María es rubio y sus ojos son verdes (*María's hair is blond and her eyes are green*).

‡ Of all the possessive adjectives, only the first person plural (nuestros/as) and the second person plural (vuestros/as) that is used in Spain (See PRONOUNS section beginning on p. 105) express gender by switching between "o" and "a" at the end.

Pronouns

Pronouns in Spanish function mostly as they do in English; they are used to replace the subject or the objects in a sentence to improve speech flow. Since they are an essential part of everyday speech, it is important to know a few things about personal pronouns in Spanish.

Subject[1]		Indirect Object		Direct Object		Reflexive Object[5]	
yo	*I*	me	*to me*	me	*me*	me	*myself*
tú	*you*	te	*to you*	te	*you*	te	*yourself*
usted[2]	*you (formal)*	le [se][4]	*to you, to him/ her, to it*	lo, la	*you (formal)*	se	*yourself, him/ herself, itself*[6]
él	*he*			lo	*him, it m.*		
ella	*she*			la	*her, it f.*		
nosotros/ as	*we*	nos	*to us*	nos	*us*	nos	*ourselves*
voso-tros/as[3]	*you pl.*	os	*to you pl.*	os	*you pl.*	os	*your-selves*
ustedes	*you pl.*	les [se]	*to you, to them*	los, las	*you pl.*	se	*your-selves, them-selves*
ellos	*they m.*			los	*them m.*		*them-selves*
ellas	*they f.*			las	*them f.*		

TABLE NOTE 1. In Spanish a verb's conjugation generally corresponds to a specific subject (see VERB CONJUGATION CHARTS section beginning on p. 108), therefore subject pronouns can be, and often are, omitted. Note that Spanish does not have an equivalent of the subject pronoun "it:"

Está lloviendo.   *It is raining.*   ¿Quién era?   *Who was it?*

TABLE NOTE 2. **Usted** *(Ud.)* is a more formal way of addressing a second person; it is used to address people of a superior rank (elders, bosses, officials, etc.) and with new acquaintances. Formal address uses the verb forms and pronouns of the third person as a way of setting a respectful distance between speaker and addressee (see VERB CONJUGATION CHARTS section beginning on p. 108). Compare the following sentences:

Formal: ¿Cómo **está** (usted)?   *How are you?*
No quiero molestar**lo**.   *I don't want to bother you.*

Informal: ¿Cómo **estás** (tú)?   *How are you?*
No quiero molestar**te**.   *I don't want to bother you.*

Usted is used systematically in Latin America where it is considered polite, but only sporadically in Spain.

TABLE NOTE 3. **Vosotros/as** and **Ustedes** are used to address a group (some English dialects use "you all" or "y'all" for the same purpose). **Vosotros/as** has its own set of verb forms and pronouns, while **ustedes** uses those of the third person plural (see VERB CONJUGATION CHARTS section beginning on p. 108). Although **ustedes** is the plural form of **usted**, no formality is necessarily implied. **Vosotros/as** is only used in Spain.

TABLE NOTE 4. Object pronouns can precede an active verb or be attached at the end of an infinitive, a gerund, or an affirmative command (see VERB section beginning on p. 112):

Quiero comer una manzana. >	**La** quiero comer. = Quiero comer**la**.
I want to eat an apple. >	*I want to eat it.*
Estoy comiendo una manzana. >	**La** estoy comiendo. = Estoy comiénd**ola**.
I am eating an apple. >	*I am eating it.*
¡Come la manzana! > ¡Cóme**la**! but	¡No comas la manzana! > ¡No **la** comas!
Eat the apple. > *Eat it.*	*Don't eat the apple.* > *Don't eat it.*

Direct objects can appear in a sentence as either a noun or a pronoun but not both. However, indirect object pronouns <u>must be used</u> whether or not the indirect object noun appears in the sentence:

Pedro **me** da dinero (a mí).   *Pedro gives money to me.*
Juan **le** da flores (a María).   *Juan gives flowers to María.*

When using two object pronouns, the indirect object pronoun <u>always</u> comes first:

Pedro **me lo** da.   *Pedro gives it to me.*

When combined with the direct object pronouns **lo, la, los,** or **las**, the indirect object pronoun **le** changes to **se**:

Juan **se las** da (a María).   *Juan gives **them to her** (to María).*

TABLE NOTE 5. As in English, **reflexive pronouns** are used to "reflect" or return the action expressed by the verb back upon the subject:

Me veo en el espejo.	*I see myself in the mirror.*
María **se** viste.	*María dresses (herself).*

Common reflexive actions include getting up (*levantarse*), washing (*lavarse*) or bathing (*bañarse*), sitting (*sentarse*), lying down (*acostarse*), and falling asleep (*dormirse*). However, as long as it makes sense, any verb can be made to describe a reflexive action by adding a reflexive pronoun. Sometimes reflexivity is added for emphasis or precision. Compare the following:

romper *to break*	Rompiste la ventana.	*You broke the window.*
romperse *to break*	Te rompiste la pierna.	*You broke your leg.*
dormir *to sleep*	Juan está durmiendo.	*Juan is sleeping.*
dormirse *to fall asleep*	Juan está durmiéndose.	*Juan is falling asleep.*
ir *to go*	Vamos al cine.	*Let's go to the movies.*
irse *to leave, to go away*	Vámonos al cine.	*Let's leave for the movies.*

Note that reflexive pronouns follow similar positioning rules as object pronouns.

TABLE NOTE 6. In Spanish the pronoun **se** is very often used to express a passive or an impersonal action in which the object may assume the function of the subject (which creates a reflexive-like expression):

En México **se** habla español.	*Spanish is spoken in Mexico. / People speak Spanish in Mexico.*
No **se** debe desperdiciar agua.	*Water mustn't be wasted. / One mustn't waste water.*

Negativity

In a negative sentence, a negative word <u>must</u> come before the verb and any preceding pronouns:

No te quiero pero **nunca** te lo había dicho.	*I do not love you but I had never told you.*

Spanish actually requires double, and even triple negatives. Negativity must be expressed throughout the sentence:

Nunca has querido a **nadie**.	*You have never loved anyone.*
Nadie quiere ir **nunca** a **ningún** lado conmigo.	*No one ever wants to go anywhere with me.*

Verb Conjugation Charts

Regular verbs, simple tenses*

Infinitive	INDICATIVE						SUBJUNCTIVE	
	Present	Preterit	Imperfect	Future	Conditional		Present	Past
hablar (*to talk*)	hablo	hablé	hablaba	hablaré	hablaría		hable	hablara
	hablas	hablaste	hablabas	hablarás	hablarías		hables	hablaras
	habla	habló	hablaba	hablará	hablaría		hable	hablara
hablando (*talking*)	hablamos	hablamos	hablábamos	hablaremos	hablaríamos		hablemos	habláramos
hablado (*talked*)	habláis	hablasteis	hablabais	hablaréis	hablaríais		habléis	hablarais
	hablan	hablaron	hablaban	hablarán	hablarían		hablen	hablaran
comer (*to eat*)	como	comí	comía	comeré	comería		coma	comiera
	comes	comiste	comías	comerás	comerías		comas	comieras
	come	comió	comía	comerá	comería		coma	comiera
comiendo (*eating*)	comemos	comimos	comíamos	comeremos	comeríamos		comamos	comiéramos
comido (*eaten*)	coméis	comisteis	comíais	comeréis	comeríais		comáis	comierais
	comen	comieron	comían	comerán	comerían		coman	comieran

vivir (to live)	vivo	viví	vivía	viviré	viviría	viva	viviera
	vives	viviste	vivías	vivirás	vivirías	vivas	vivieras
	vive	vivió	vivía	vivirá	viviría	viva	viviera
viviendo (living)	vivimos	vivimos	vivíamos	viviremos	viviríamos	vivamos	viviéramos
vivido (lived)	vivís	vivisteis	vivíais	viviréis	viviríais	viváis	viviereis
	viven	vivieron	vivían	vivirán	vivirían	vivan	vivieran

Regular verbs, perfect tenses‡

INDICATIVE							
Present Perfect		Past Perfect		Future Perfect		Conditional Perfect	
he	hablado	había	hablado	habré	hablado	habría	hablado
has	comido	habías	comido	habrás	comido	habrías	comido
ha	vivido	había	vivido	habrá	vivido	habría	vivido
hemos		habíamos		habremos		habríamos	
habéis		habíais		habréis		habríais	
han		habían		habrán		habrían	

SUBJUNCTIVE			
Present Perfect		Past Perfect	
haya	hablado	hubiera	hablado
hayas	comido	hubieras	comido
haya	vivido	hubiera	vivido
hayamos		hubiéramos	
hayáis		hubierais	
hayan		hubieran	

---

* Regular verbs are predictable; note the patterns of the different tenses to master verb conjugation quickly.

‡ As in English, perfect tenses in Spanish use the helping verb *haber* (to have): yo **he** hablado (*I have talked*); tu **habías** comido (*you had eaten*). However, note that to indicate possession Spanish uses the verb *tener* (to have).

Some common irregular verbs, simple tenses

Infinitive & Participles	INDICATIVE						SUBJUNCTIVE	
	Present	Preterit	Imperfect	Future	Conditional		Present	Past
estar (*to be*)	estoy	estuve	estaba	estaré	estaría		esté	estuviera
	estás	estuviste	estabas	estarás	estarías		estés	estuvieras
	está	estuvo	estaba	estará	estaría		esté	estuviera
estando (*being*)	estamos	estuvimos	estábamos	estaremos	estaríamos		estemos	estuviéramos
estado (*been*)	estáis	estuvisteis	estabais	estaréis	estaríais		estéis	estuvierais
	están	estuvieron	estaban	estarán	estarían		estén	estuvieran
dar (*to give*)	doy	di	daba	daré	daría		dé	diera
	das	diste	dabas	darás	darías		des	dieras
	da	dio	daba	dará	daría		dé	diera
dando (*giving*)	damos	dimos	dábamos	daremos	daríamos		demos	diéramos
dado (*given*)	dáis	disteis	dabais	daréis	daríais		deis	dierais
	dan	dieron	daban	darán	darían		den	dieran
hacer (*to do, to make*)	hago	hice	hacía	haré	haría		haga	hiciera
	haces	hiciste	hacías	harás	harías		hagas	hicieras
	hace	hizo	hacía	hará	haría		haga	hiciera
	hacemos	hicimos	hacíamos	haremos	haríamos		hagamos	hiciéramos
haciendo (*making*)	hacéis	hicisteis	hacíais	haréis	haríais		hagáis	hicierais
hecho (*made*)	hacen	hicieron	hacían	harán	harían		hagan	hicieran

ir (*to go*) / **yendo** (*going*) / **ido** (*gone*)

voy	fui	iba	iré	iría	vaya	fuera
vas	fuiste	ibas	irás	irías	vayas	fueras
va	fue	iba	irá	iría	vaya	fuera
vamos	fuimos	íbamos	iremos	iríamos	vayamos	fuéramos
vais	fuisteis	ibais	iréis	iríais	vayáis	fuerais
van	fueron	iban	irán	irían	vayan	fueran

ser (*to be*) / **siendo** (*being*) / **sido** (*been*)

soy	fui †	era	seré	sería	sea	fuera
eres	fuiste	eras	serás	serías	seas	fueras
es	fue	era	será	seria	sea	fuera
somos	fuimos	éramos	seremos	seríamos	seamos	fuéramos
sois	fuisteis	erais	seréis	seríais	seáis	fuerais
son	fueron	eran	serán	serían	sean	fueran

venir (*to come*) / **viniendo** (*coming*) / **venido** (*come*)

vengo	vine	venía	vendré	vendría	venga	viniera
vienes	viniste	venías	vendrás	vendrías	vengas	vinieras
viene	vino	venía	vendrá	vendría	venga	viniera
venimos	vinimos	veníamos	vendremos	vendríamos	vengamos	viniéramos
venís	vinisteis	veníais	vendréis	vendríais	vengáis	viniereis
vienen	vinieron	venían	vendrán	vendrían	vengan	vinieran

† The verbs *ser* and *ir* share the preterit and past subjunctive tenses; context determines which verb is being used.

Verbs, Tenses, and Moods

Ser vs. Estar

English translates both the verb *ser* and the verb *estar* as "to be." However, in Spanish they have very different meanings. *Ser* is used to talk about essences (aspects that are perceived as being inherent to or definitive of the subject) and about time. *Estar* is used to talk about states (aspects or conditions that are merely circumstantial to the subject) and about location (space). Compare the following sentences:

Pedro **es** un tipo simpático pero hoy **está** enojado.	*Pedro is a nice guy but today he is angry.*
Son las dos y María todavía **está** dormida.*	*It is two o'clock and María is still asleep.*
La casa que **está** en esa colina **es** amarilla.	*The house that is on that hill is yellow.*
La fiesta **fue** en la casa que **está** en venta.†	*The party was at the house that is for sale.*

The verb *estar* is used in combination with a gerund to form progressive tenses:

Estoy escribiendo en la computadora.	*I am writing on the computer.*
Estábamos pensando en llamarte.	*We were thinking about calling you.*

Verbs like gustar

The verb *gustar* is generally, and accurately, translated as "to like":

A Juan **le gustan** los postres.	*Juan likes desserts.*

In Spanish, however, Juan is not the subject of the verb *gustan* but its indirect object, while *los postres* functions as both subject and direct object. Note that the verb agrees with *los postres* and that *le* agrees

---

* States can be permanent. In Spanish, death is considered a state: Las plantas de mi casa **están** muertas (*My house plants are dead*).
† Since events involve a lot more than their location, the verb *ser* is used to talk about parties and ceremonies in general: la boda **será** en la catedral (*The wedding will be in the cathedral*).

with Juan. Therefore, a more literal translation would be: "Desserts are pleasing to Juan." There are a number of verbs that function like *gustar*. Consider the following examples:

María **le gusta** a Pedro.*	*Pedro likes María. (lit. María is pleasing to Pedro.)*
(A Ana y a Luis) No **les interesa** la ciencia.†	*Science doesn't interest them (Ana and Luis).*
(A mí) **Me preocupa** llegar tarde a mi cita.	*Being late for my appointment worries me.*

Other common verbs that function like *gustar* include *encantar* (to really like), *importar* (to matter), *aburrir* (to bore), *quedar* (to have left), *faltar* (to lack), and *doler* (to hurt). It is interesting to note that this type of verb generally expresses subjective perceptions and is used to talk about things the subject finds pleasing, boring, important, or painful.

Preterit vs. Imperfect

The preterit tense is used when a past action is considered singular and definitely concluded:

Pasé un mes en Madrid el año pasado.	*I spent a month in Madrid last year.*
Fue entonces cuando **conocí** a Juan.	*It was then that I met Juan.*

The imperfect tense is used for recurring actions in the past or actions which happened over an indefinite period of time in the past:

Antes, **iba** a Madrid cada año.	*Before, I used to go to Madrid every year.*
En esa época, Juan **estudiaba** leyes.	*At the time, Juan studied (was studying) law.*

---

* In Spanish object nouns can precede the verb; the preposition "*a*" is used to avoid confusion when two possible agents are involved (i.e., Mary might be the one who likes Pedro).
† The indirect-object pronoun is necessary, but the indirect object itself may be omitted or included to add precision to the sentence.

The preterit and the imperfect are often combined in a sentence to emphasize certain actions (preterit) over others that provide context or serve as backdrop (imperfect):

Decidí comer mientras te **esperaba.**   *I decided to eat lunch while I waited (was waiting) for you.*

Llovía cuando **llegó** el avión.   *It was raining when the plane arrived.*

Subjunctive mood

In Spanish, the subjunctive mood is used to express possibility, uncertainty, and empathy. When speaking about actions that happen in the present, happened in the past, or will happen in the future, the indicative mood is used. For talking about actions which may (or may not) happen, or may (or may not) have happened, the subjunctive mood is used. In general, the subjunctive is used to talk about situations that are beyond the control of a sentence's primary subject. For instance, we may say that it is important, necessary even, for drivers to come to a full stop at a stop sign which, however, does not guarantee that they will. Likewise, even if Juan wanted Pedro to lend him money, Pedro might have refused. Finally, a person may feel sorry about another's tragedy, but be unable to do anything to change it. Consider the following examples:

Es posible que **vaya** a México en verano.*
It is possible that I will go to Mexico in the summer.

Es importante (necesario) que los conductores **respeten** las señales de tránsito.
It is important (necessary) that drivers respect traffic signals.

Juan quería que Pedro le **prestara** dinero.†
Juan wanted Pedro to lend him money.

---

* A subjunctive clause depends, at least implicitly, on an indicative statement; they are linked by a conjunctive element, most often "*que*." In other words, possibility must always be grounded in reality.
† Generally, if the verb in the main clause is in the present tense, the verb in the subjunctive clause will also be in the present. Likewise, a past-tense verb in the main clause calls for the past tense in the subjunctive clause.

Siento que **hayas perdido** tu vuelo.
I am sorry that you (have) missed your flight.

In Spanish *pensar* (to think) and *creer* (to believe) express certainty on the part of the primary subject. Therefore, the subjunctive is unnecessary. However, lack of belief does not rule out possibility altogether; therefore the subjunctive is appropriate. Compare the following sentences:

María **cree** (**piensa**) que existen los fantasmas, pero yo **no pienso** (**creo**) que existan.
María believes (thinks) ghosts exist, but I don't think (believe) that they do.

When a single subject is involved in the action there is no need to introduce a subjunctive clause; the verb in the infinitive is used in the main clause instead. Compare the following sentences:

Quiero que (tú) **aprendas** español.   *I want you to learn Spanish*
Quiero **aprender** español.   *I want to learn Spanish.*

Commands and requests

	Affirmative commands	Negative commands
Informal commands	habla (*talk*)	no hables (*don't talk*)
	come (*eat*)	no comas (*don't eat*)
	siént**ate** (*sit down*)	no **te** sientes (*don't sit down*)
Formal commands (requests)	hable (*talk*)	no hable (*don't talk*)
	coma (*eat*)	no coma (*don't eat*)
	siént**ese** (*sit down*)	no **se** siente (*don't sit down*)

Commands can be affirmative or negative. In Spanish they can also be formal or informal. Informal commands are directed at someone whom the speaker would address as "*tú*" (a child, a family member, a good friend, etc.). On the other hand, formal commands are directed toward someone who would be addressed as "*usted*" such as an elder, a teacher, an officer, the president, a new acquaintance, etc. (see PRONOUNS section beginning on p. 105).

Note that formal commands use subjunctive verb forms as if implying the possibility of refusal on the part of the addressee (see VERB CONJUGATION CHARTS beginning on p. 108). In that sense, formal affirmative commands are more like requests. Likewise, since there is no guarantee that a negative command will be carried out, subjunctive forms are also used.

Commands and requests can also be addressed to a group:

	Affirmative commands	Negative commands
Nosotros commands	hablemos (*let's talk*)	no hablemos (*let's not talk*)
	comamos (*let's eat*)	no comamos (*let's not eat*)
	sentémonos (*let's sit down*)‡	no nos sentemos (*let's not sit down*)
Vosotros commands	hablad (*talk*)	no habléis (*don't talk*)
	comed (*eat*)	no comáis (*don't eat*)
	sentaos (*sit down*)*	no os sentéis (*don't sit down*)
Ustedes commands	hablen (*talk*)	no hablen (*don't talk*)
	coman (*eat*)	no coman (*don't eat*)
	siéntense (*sit down*)	no se sienten (*don't sit down*)

‡ Note the dropping of the "s" in reflexive-verb *nosotros* commands.
* Note the dropping of the "d" in reflexive-verb *vosotros* commands.

Prepositions

Prepositions in any language can seem arbitrary—in English people can ride **in** a car or **on** a bus. However, there are a few general guidelines for using the most common prepositions in Spanish:

a (*to*) conveys the sense of going toward something. Actions such as going somewhere, beginning or learning something, and giving something to someone use the preposition **a**:

Vamos **a** la escuela para empezar **a** aprender **a** hablar español.
Let's go to school in order to begin learning to speak Spanish.

de (*of, from*) conveys the sense of coming or stemming from somewhere. The preposition **de** can express provenance, origin, material, and belonging:

La madera **de** la mesa **de** madera **de** Juan viene **de** la selva **de** Guatemala.
The wood that Juan's wooden table is made of comes from the jungle of Guatemala.

en (*in, on, at*) expresses location in general:

En la universidad, los libros están **en** repisas **en** la biblioteca.
At the university, the books are on shelves in the library.

con (*with*) expresses addition, instrumentality, and accompaniment:

Me gusta comer fresas **con** crema **con** una cuchara **con** mis amigos.
I like to eat strawberries with cream with a spoon with my friends.

por (*for, because of, around, through, by*) indicates the cause or the reason behind an action, as well as motion, passage, means, and exchange.

Vamos a hacer un viaje **por** barco **por** el Caribe **por** tres semanas; pagué mil dólares **por** él.
We're going on a trip around the Caribbean by boat for three weeks; I paid $1,000 dollars for it.

para (*for, to, in order to, by*) specifies the recipient or the purpose of an action, as well as a direction, a destination, or a deadline.

El regalo **para** mi mamá estará listo **para** mañana; es una caja **para** guardar sus joyas.
The present for my mom will be ready by tomorrow; it's a box for storing her jewelry.

The use of prepositions in English doesn't always match Spanish use. In some cases, English needs a preposition where Spanish does not:

Juan se enamoró **de** María.	*Juan fell in love **with** María.*
Puedes contar **con** nosotros.	*You can count **on** us.*
Estoy buscando algo especial.	*I'm looking **for** something special.*

In Spanish a preposition can never be placed at the end of a phrase.

Index

A CATALOG OF SELECTED DOVER BOOKS IN ALL FIELDS OF INTEREST

100 BEST-LOVED POEMS, Edited by Philip Smith. "The Passionate Shepherd to His Love," "Shall I compare thee to a summer's day?" "Death, be not proud," "The Raven," "The Road Not Taken," plus works by Blake, Wordsworth, Byron, Shelley, Keats, many others. 96pp. 5³⁄₁₆ x 8¼. 0-486-28553-7

100 SMALL HOUSES OF THE THIRTIES, Brown-Blodgett Company. Exterior photographs and floor plans for 100 charming structures. Illustrations of models accompanied by descriptions of interiors, color schemes, closet space, and other amenities. 200 illustrations. 112pp. 8⅜ x 11. 0-486-44131-8

1000 TURN-OF-THE-CENTURY HOUSES: With Illustrations and Floor Plans, Herbert C. Chivers. Reproduced from a rare edition, this showcase of homes ranges from cottages and bungalows to sprawling mansions. Each house is meticulously illustrated and accompanied by complete floor plans. 256pp. 9⅜ x 12¼. 0-486-45596-3

101 GREAT AMERICAN POEMS, Edited by The American Poetry & Literacy Project. Rich treasury of verse from the 19th and 20th centuries includes works by Edgar Allan Poe, Robert Frost, Walt Whitman, Langston Hughes, Emily Dickinson, T. S. Eliot, other notables. 96pp. 5³⁄₁₆ x 8¼. 0-486-40158-8

101 GREAT SAMURAI PRINTS, Utagawa Kuniyoshi. Kuniyoshi was a master of the warrior woodblock print — and these 18th-century illustrations represent the pinnacle of his craft. Full-color portraits of renowned Japanese samurais pulse with movement, passion, and remarkably fine detail. 112pp. 8⅜ x 11. 0-486-46523-3

ABC OF BALLET, Janet Grosser. Clearly worded, abundantly illustrated little guide defines basic ballet-related terms: arabesque, battement, pas de chat, relevé, sissonne, many others. Pronunciation guide included. Excellent primer. 48pp. 4³⁄₁₆ x 5¾. 0-486-40871-X

ACCESSORIES OF DRESS: An Illustrated Encyclopedia, Katherine Lester and Bess Viola Oerke. Illustrations of hats, veils, wigs, cravats, shawls, shoes, gloves, and other accessories enhance an engaging commentary that reveals the humor and charm of the many-sided story of accessorized apparel. 644 figures and 59 plates. 608pp. 6 ⅛ x 9¼. 0-486-43378-1

ADVENTURES OF HUCKLEBERRY FINN, Mark Twain. Join Huck and Jim as their boyhood adventures along the Mississippi River lead them into a world of excitement, danger, and self-discovery. Humorous narrative, lyrical descriptions of the Mississippi valley, and memorable characters. 224pp. 5³⁄₁₆ x 8¼. 0-486-28061-6

ALICE STARMORE'S BOOK OF FAIR ISLE KNITTING, Alice Starmore. A noted designer from the region of Scotland's Fair Isle explores the history and techniques of this distinctive, stranded-color knitting style and provides copious illustrated instructions for 14 original knitwear designs. 208pp. 8⅜ x 10⅞. 0-486-47218-3

ALICE'S ADVENTURES IN WONDERLAND, Lewis Carroll. Beloved classic about a little girl lost in a topsy-turvy land and her encounters with the White Rabbit, March Hare, Mad Hatter, Cheshire Cat, and other delightfully improbable characters. 42 illustrations by Sir John Tenniel. 96pp. 5³⁄₁₆ x 8¼. 0-486-27543-4

AMERICA'S LIGHTHOUSES: An Illustrated History, Francis Ross Holland. Profusely illustrated fact-filled survey of American lighthouses since 1716. Over 200 stations — East, Gulf, and West coasts, Great Lakes, Hawaii, Alaska, Puerto Rico, the Virgin Islands, and the Mississippi and St. Lawrence Rivers. 240pp. 8 x 10¾. 0-486-25576-X

AN ENCYCLOPEDIA OF THE VIOLIN, Alberto Bachmann. Translated by Frederick H. Martens. Introduction by Eugene Ysaye. First published in 1925, this renowned reference remains unsurpassed as a source of essential information, from construction and evolution to repertoire and technique. Includes a glossary and 73 illustrations. 496pp. 6⅛ x 9¼. 0-486-46618-3

ANIMALS: 1,419 Copyright-Free Illustrations of Mammals, Birds, Fish, Insects, etc., Selected by Jim Harter. Selected for its visual impact and ease of use, this outstanding collection of wood engravings presents over 1,000 species of animals in extremely lifelike poses. Includes mammals, birds, reptiles, amphibians, fish, insects, and other invertebrates. 284pp. 9 x 12. 0-486-23766-4

THE ANNALS, Tacitus. Translated by Alfred John Church and William Jackson Brodribb. This vital chronicle of Imperial Rome, written by the era's great historian, spans A.D. 14-68 and paints incisive psychological portraits of major figures, from Tiberius to Nero. 416pp. 5³⁄₁₆ x 8¼. 0-486-45236-0

ANTIGONE, Sophocles. Filled with passionate speeches and sensitive probing of moral and philosophical issues, this powerful and often-performed Greek drama reveals the grim fate that befalls the children of Oedipus. Footnotes. 64pp. 5³⁄₁₆ x 8 ¼. 0-486-27804-2

ART DECO DECORATIVE PATTERNS IN FULL COLOR, Christian Stoll. Reprinted from a rare 1910 portfolio, 160 sensuous and exotic images depict a breathtaking array of florals, geometrics, and abstracts — all elegant in their stark simplicity. 64pp. 8⅜ x 11. 0-486-44862-2

THE ARTHUR RACKHAM TREASURY: 86 Full-Color Illustrations, Arthur Rackham. Selected and Edited by Jeff A. Menges. A stunning treasury of 86 full-page plates span the famed English artist's career, from *Rip Van Winkle* (1905) to masterworks such as *Undine, A Midsummer Night's Dream,* and *Wind in the Willows* (1939). 96pp. 8⅜ x 11. 0-486-44685-9

THE AUTHENTIC GILBERT & SULLIVAN SONGBOOK, W. S. Gilbert and A. S. Sullivan. The most comprehensive collection available, this songbook includes selections from every one of Gilbert and Sullivan's light operas. Ninety-two numbers are presented uncut and unedited, and in their original keys. 410pp. 9 x 12. 0-486-23482-7

THE AWAKENING, Kate Chopin. First published in 1899, this controversial novel of a New Orleans wife's search for love outside a stifling marriage shocked readers. Today, it remains a first-rate narrative with superb characterization. New introductory Note. 128pp. 5³⁄₁₆ x 8¼. 0-486-27786-0

BASIC DRAWING, Louis Priscilla. Beginning with perspective, this commonsense manual progresses to the figure in movement, light and shade, anatomy, drapery, composition, trees and landscape, and outdoor sketching. Black-and-white illustrations throughout. 128pp. 8⅜ x 11. 0-486-45815-6

THE BATTLES THAT CHANGED HISTORY, Fletcher Pratt. Historian profiles 16 crucial conflicts, ancient to modern, that changed the course of Western civilization. Gripping accounts of battles led by Alexander the Great, Joan of Arc, Ulysses S. Grant, other commanders. 27 maps. 352pp. 5⅜ x 8½. 0-486-41129-X

BEETHOVEN'S LETTERS, Ludwig van Beethoven. Edited by Dr. A. C. Kalischer. Features 457 letters to fellow musicians, friends, greats, patrons, and literary men. Reveals musical thoughts, quirks of personality, insights, and daily events. Includes 15 plates. 410pp. 5⅜ x 8½. 0-486-22769-3

BERNICE BOBS HER HAIR AND OTHER STORIES, F. Scott Fitzgerald. This brilliant anthology includes 6 of Fitzgerald's most popular stories: "The Diamond as Big as the Ritz," the title tale, "The Offshore Pirate," "The Ice Palace," "The Jelly Bean," and "May Day." 176pp. 5⅜ x 8½. 0-486-47049-0

BESLER'S BOOK OF FLOWERS AND PLANTS: 73 Full-Color Plates from Hortus Eystettensis, 1613, Basilius Besler. Here is a selection of magnificent plates from the *Hortus Eystettensis,* which vividly illustrated and identified the plants, flowers, and trees that thrived in the legendary German garden at Eichstätt. 80pp. 8⅜ x 11. 0-486-46005-3

THE BOOK OF KELLS, Edited by Blanche Cirker. Painstakingly reproduced from a rare facsimile edition, this volume contains full-page decorations, portraits, illustrations, plus a sampling of textual leaves with exquisite calligraphy and ornamentation. 32 full-color illustrations. 32pp. 9⅜ x 12¼. 0-486-24345-1

THE BOOK OF THE CROSSBOW: With an Additional Section on Catapults and Other Siege Engines, Ralph Payne-Gallwey. Fascinating study traces history and use of crossbow as military and sporting weapon, from Middle Ages to modern times. Also covers related weapons: balistas, catapults, Turkish bows, more. Over 240 illustrations. 400pp. 7¼ x 10⅛. 0-486-28720-3

THE BUNGALOW BOOK: Floor Plans and Photos of 112 Houses, 1910, Henry L. Wilson. Here are 112 of the most popular and economic blueprints of the early 20th century — plus an illustration or photograph of each completed house. A wonderful time capsule that still offers a wealth of valuable insights. 160pp. 8⅜ x 11. 0-486-45104-6

THE CALL OF THE WILD, Jack London. A classic novel of adventure, drawn from London's own experiences as a Klondike adventurer, relating the story of a heroic dog caught in the brutal life of the Alaska Gold Rush. Note. 64pp. 5³⁄₁₆ x 8¼. 0-486-26472-6

CANDIDE, Voltaire. Edited by Francois-Marie Arouet. One of the world's great satires since its first publication in 1759. Witty, caustic skewering of romance, science, philosophy, religion, government — nearly all human ideals and institutions. 112pp. 5³⁄₁₆ x 8¼. 0-486-26689-3

CELEBRATED IN THEIR TIME: Photographic Portraits from the George Grantham Bain Collection, Edited by Amy Pastan. With an Introduction by Michael Carlebach. Remarkable portrait gallery features 112 rare images of Albert Einstein, Charlie Chaplin, the Wright Brothers, Henry Ford, and other luminaries from the worlds of politics, art, entertainment, and industry. 128pp. 8⅜ x 11. 0-486-46754-6

CHARIOTS FOR APOLLO: The NASA History of Manned Lunar Spacecraft to 1969, Courtney G. Brooks, James M. Grimwood, and Loyd S. Swenson, Jr. This illustrated history by a trio of experts is the definitive reference on the Apollo spacecraft and lunar modules. It traces the vehicles' design, development, and operation in space. More than 100 photographs and illustrations. 576pp. 6¾ x 9¼. 0-486-46756-2

Browse over 9,000 books at www.doverpublications.com

A CHRISTMAS CAROL, Charles Dickens. This engrossing tale relates Ebenezer Scrooge's ghostly journeys through Christmases past, present, and future and his ultimate transformation from a harsh and grasping old miser to a charitable and compassionate human being. 80pp. 5³⁄₁₆ x 8¼. 0-486-26865-9

COMMON SENSE, Thomas Paine. First published in January of 1776, this highly influential landmark document clearly and persuasively argued for American separation from Great Britain and paved the way for the Declaration of Independence. 64pp. 5³⁄₁₆ x 8¼. 0-486-29602-4

THE COMPLETE SHORT STORIES OF OSCAR WILDE, Oscar Wilde. Complete texts of "The Happy Prince and Other Tales," "A House of Pomegranates," "Lord Arthur Savile's Crime and Other Stories," "Poems in Prose," and "The Portrait of Mr. W. H." 208pp. 5³⁄₁₆ x 8¼. 0-486-45216-6

COMPLETE SONNETS, William Shakespeare. Over 150 exquisite poems deal with love, friendship, the tyranny of time, beauty's evanescence, death, and other themes in language of remarkable power, precision, and beauty. Glossary of archaic terms. 80pp. 5³⁄₁₆ x 8¼. 0-486-26686-9

THE COUNT OF MONTE CRISTO: Abridged Edition, Alexandre Dumas. Falsely accused of treason, Edmond Dantès is imprisoned in the bleak Chateau d'If. After a hair-raising escape, he launches an elaborate plot to extract a bitter revenge against those who betrayed him. 448pp. 5³⁄₁₆ x 8¼. 0-486-45643-9

CRAFTSMAN BUNGALOWS: Designs from the Pacific Northwest, Yoho & Merritt. This reprint of a rare catalog, showcasing the charming simplicity and cozy style of Craftsman bungalows, is filled with photos of completed homes, plus floor plans and estimated costs. An indispensable resource for architects, historians, and illustrators. 112pp. 10 x 7. 0-486-46875-5

CRAFTSMAN BUNGALOWS: 59 Homes from "The Craftsman," Edited by Gustav Stickley. Best and most attractive designs from Arts and Crafts Movement publication — 1903–1916 — includes sketches, photographs of homes, floor plans, descriptive text. 128pp. 8¼ x 11. 0-486-25829-7

CRIME AND PUNISHMENT, Fyodor Dostoyevsky. Translated by Constance Garnett. Supreme masterpiece tells the story of Raskolnikov, a student tormented by his own thoughts after he murders an old woman. Overwhelmed by guilt and terror, he confesses and goes to prison. 480pp. 5³⁄₁₆ x 8¼. 0-486-41587-2

THE DECLARATION OF INDEPENDENCE AND OTHER GREAT DOCUMENTS OF AMERICAN HISTORY: 1775-1865, Edited by John Grafton. Thirteen compelling and influential documents: Henry's "Give Me Liberty or Give Me Death," Declaration of Independence, The Constitution, Washington's First Inaugural Address, The Monroe Doctrine, The Emancipation Proclamation, Gettysburg Address, more. 64pp. 5³⁄₁₆ x 8¼. 0-486-41124-9

THE DESERT AND THE SOWN: Travels in Palestine and Syria, Gertrude Bell. "The female Lawrence of Arabia," Gertrude Bell wrote captivating, perceptive accounts of her travels in the Middle East. This intriguing narrative, accompanied by 160 photos, traces her 1905 sojourn in Lebanon, Syria, and Palestine. 368pp. 5⅜ x 8½. 0-486-46876-3

A DOLL'S HOUSE, Henrik Ibsen. Ibsen's best-known play displays his genius for realistic prose drama. An expression of women's rights, the play climaxes when the central character, Nora, rejects a smothering marriage and life in "a doll's house." 80pp. 5³⁄₁₆ x 8¼. 0-486-27062-9

DOOMED SHIPS: Great Ocean Liner Disasters, William H. Miller, Jr. Nearly 200 photographs, many from private collections, highlight tales of some of the vessels whose pleasure cruises ended in catastrophe: the *Morro Castle, Normandie, Andrea Doria, Europa,* and many others. 128pp. 8⅞ x 11¼. 0-486-45366-9

THE DORÉ BIBLE ILLUSTRATIONS, Gustave Doré. Detailed plates from the Bible: the Creation scenes, Adam and Eve, horrifying visions of the Flood, the battle sequences with their monumental crowds, depictions of the life of Jesus, 241 plates in all. 241pp. 9 x 12. 0-486-23004-X

DRAWING DRAPERY FROM HEAD TO TOE, Cliff Young. Expert guidance on how to draw shirts, pants, skirts, gloves, hats, and coats on the human figure, including folds in relation to the body, pull and crush, action folds, creases, more. Over 200 drawings. 48pp. 8¼ x 11. 0-486-45591-2

DUBLINERS, James Joyce. A fine and accessible introduction to the work of one of the 20th century's most influential writers, this collection features 15 tales, including a masterpiece of the short-story genre, "The Dead." 160pp. 5³⁄₁₆ x 8¼.
0-486-26870-5

EASY-TO-MAKE POP-UPS, Joan Irvine. Illustrated by Barbara Reid. Dozens of wonderful ideas for three-dimensional paper fun — from holiday greeting cards with moving parts to a pop-up menagerie. Easy-to-follow, illustrated instructions for more than 30 projects. 299 black-and-white illustrations. 96pp. 8⅝ x 11.
0-486-44622-0

EASY-TO-MAKE STORYBOOK DOLLS: A "Novel" Approach to Cloth Dollmaking, Sherralyn St. Clair. Favorite fictional characters come alive in this unique beginner's dollmaking guide. Includes patterns for Pollyanna, Dorothy from *The Wonderful Wizard of Oz,* Mary of *The Secret Garden,* plus easy-to-follow instructions, 263 black-and-white illustrations, and an 8-page color insert. 112pp. 8¼ x 11. 0-486-47360-0

EINSTEIN'S ESSAYS IN SCIENCE, Albert Einstein. Speeches and essays in accessible, everyday language profile influential physicists such as Niels Bohr and Isaac Newton. They also explore areas of physics to which the author made major contributions. 128pp. 5 x 8. 0-486-47011-3

EL DORADO: Further Adventures of the Scarlet Pimpernel, Baroness Orczy. A popular sequel to *The Scarlet Pimpernel,* this suspenseful story recounts the Pimpernel's attempts to rescue the Dauphin from imprisonment during the French Revolution. An irresistible blend of intrigue, period detail, and vibrant characterizations. 352pp. 5³⁄₁₆ x 8¼. 0-486-44026-5

ELEGANT SMALL HOMES OF THE TWENTIES: 99 Designs from a Competition, Chicago Tribune. Nearly 100 designs for five- and six-room houses feature New England and Southern colonials, Normandy cottages, stately Italianate dwellings, and other fascinating snapshots of American domestic architecture of the 1920s. 112pp. 9 x 12. 0-486-46910-7

THE ELEMENTS OF STYLE: The Original Edition, William Strunk, Jr. This is the book that generations of writers have relied upon for timeless advice on grammar, diction, syntax, and other essentials. In concise terms, it identifies the principal requirements of proper style and common errors. 64pp. 5⅜ x 8½. 0-486-44798-7

THE ELUSIVE PIMPERNEL, Baroness Orczy. Robespierre's revolutionaries find their wicked schemes thwarted by the heroic Pimpernel — Sir Percival Blakeney. In this thrilling sequel, Chauvelin devises a plot to eliminate the Pimpernel and his wife. 272pp. 5³⁄₁₆ x 8¼. 0-486-45464-9

AN ENCYCLOPEDIA OF BATTLES: Accounts of Over 1,560 Battles from 1479 B.C. to the Present, David Eggenberger. Essential details of every major battle in recorded history from the first battle of Megiddo in 1479 B.C. to Grenada in 1984. List of battle maps. 99 illustrations. 544pp. 6½ x 9¼. 0-486-24913-1

ENCYCLOPEDIA OF EMBROIDERY STITCHES, INCLUDING CREWEL, Marion Nichols. Precise explanations and instructions, clearly illustrated, on how to work chain, back, cross, knotted, woven stitches, and many more — 178 in all, including Cable Outline, Whipped Satin, and Eyelet Buttonhole. Over 1400 illustrations. 219pp. 8⅜ x 11¼. 0-486-22929-7

ENTER JEEVES: 15 Early Stories, P. G. Wodehouse. Splendid collection contains first 8 stories featuring Bertie Wooster, the deliciously dim aristocrat and Jeeves, his brainy, imperturbable manservant. Also, the complete Reggie Pepper (Bertie's prototype) series. 288pp. 5⅜ x 8½. 0-486-29717-9

ERIC SLOANE'S AMERICA: Paintings in Oil, Michael Wigley. With a Foreword by Mimi Sloane. Eric Sloane's evocative oils of America's landscape and material culture shimmer with immense historical and nostalgic appeal. This original hardcover collection gathers nearly a hundred of his finest paintings, with subjects ranging from New England to the American Southwest. 128pp. 10⅝ x 9. 0-486-46525-X

ETHAN FROME, Edith Wharton. Classic story of wasted lives, set against a bleak New England background. Superbly delineated characters in a hauntingly grim tale of thwarted love. Considered by many to be Wharton's masterpiece. 96pp. 5³⁄₁₆ x 8 ¼. 0-486-26690-7

THE EVERLASTING MAN, G. K. Chesterton. Chesterton's view of Christianity — as a blend of philosophy and mythology, satisfying intellect and spirit — applies to his brilliant book, which appeals to readers' heads as well as their hearts. 288pp. 5⅜ x 8½. 0-486-46036-3

THE FIELD AND FOREST HANDY BOOK, Daniel Beard. Written by a co-founder of the Boy Scouts, this appealing guide offers illustrated instructions for building kites, birdhouses, boats, igloos, and other fun projects, plus numerous helpful tips for campers. 448pp. 5³⁄₁₆ x 8¼. 0-486-46191-2

FINDING YOUR WAY WITHOUT MAP OR COMPASS, Harold Gatty. Useful, instructive manual shows would-be explorers, hikers, bikers, scouts, sailors, and survivalists how to find their way outdoors by observing animals, weather patterns, shifting sands, and other elements of nature. 288pp. 5⅜ x 8½. 0-486-40613-X

FIRST FRENCH READER: A Beginner's Dual-Language Book, Edited and Translated by Stanley Appelbaum. This anthology introduces 50 legendary writers — Voltaire, Balzac, Baudelaire, Proust, more — through passages from *The Red and the Black, Les Misérables, Madame Bovary,* and other classics. Original French text plus English translation on facing pages. 240pp. 5⅜ x 8½. 0-486-46178-5

FIRST GERMAN READER: A Beginner's Dual-Language Book, Edited by Harry Steinhauer. Specially chosen for their power to evoke German life and culture, these short, simple readings include poems, stories, essays, and anecdotes by Goethe, Hesse, Heine, Schiller, and others. 224pp. 5⅜ x 8½. 0-486-46179-3

FIRST SPANISH READER: A Beginner's Dual-Language Book, Angel Flores. Delightful stories, other material based on works of Don Juan Manuel, Luis Taboada, Ricardo Palma, other noted writers. Complete faithful English translations on facing pages. Exercises. 176pp. 5⅜ x 8½. 0-486-25810-6

FIVE ACRES AND INDEPENDENCE, Maurice G. Kains. Great back-to-the-land classic explains basics of self-sufficient farming. The one book to get. 95 illustrations. 397pp. 5⅜ x 8½. 0-486-20974-1

FLAGG'S SMALL HOUSES: Their Economic Design and Construction, 1922, Ernest Flagg. Although most famous for his skyscrapers, Flagg was also a proponent of the well-designed single-family dwelling. His classic treatise features innovations that save space, materials, and cost. 526 illustrations. 160pp. 9⅜ x 12¼. 0-486-45197-6

FLATLAND: A Romance of Many Dimensions, Edwin A. Abbott. Classic of science (and mathematical) fiction — charmingly illustrated by the author — describes the adventures of A. Square, a resident of Flatland, in Spaceland (three dimensions), Lineland (one dimension), and Pointland (no dimensions). 96pp. 5³⁄₁₆ x 8¼. 0-486-27263-X

FRANKENSTEIN, Mary Shelley. The story of Victor Frankenstein's monstrous creation and the havoc it caused has enthralled generations of readers and inspired countless writers of horror and suspense. With the author's own 1831 introduction. 176pp. 5³⁄₁₆ x 8¼. 0-486-28211-2

THE GARGOYLE BOOK: 572 Examples from Gothic Architecture, Lester Burbank Bridaham. Dispelling the conventional wisdom that French Gothic architectural flourishes were born of despair or gloom, Bridaham reveals the whimsical nature of these creations and the ingenious artisans who made them. 572 illustrations. 224pp. 8⅜ x 11. 0-486-44754-5

THE GIFT OF THE MAGI AND OTHER SHORT STORIES, O. Henry. Sixteen captivating stories by one of America's most popular storytellers. Included are such classics as "The Gift of the Magi," "The Last Leaf," and "The Ransom of Red Chief." Publisher's Note. 96pp. 5³⁄₁₆ x 8¼. 0-486-27061-0

THE GOETHE TREASURY: Selected Prose and Poetry, Johann Wolfgang von Goethe. Edited, Selected, and with an Introduction by Thomas Mann. In addition to his lyric poetry, Goethe wrote travel sketches, autobiographical studies, essays, letters, and proverbs in rhyme and prose. This collection presents outstanding examples from each genre. 368pp. 5⅜ x 8½. 0-486-44780-4

GREAT EXPECTATIONS, Charles Dickens. Orphaned Pip is apprenticed to the dirty work of the forge but dreams of becoming a gentleman — and one day finds himself in possession of "great expectations." Dickens' finest novel. 400pp. 5³⁄₁₆ x 8¼. 0-486-41586-4

GREAT WRITERS ON THE ART OF FICTION: From Mark Twain to Joyce Carol Oates, Edited by James Daley. An indispensable source of advice and inspiration, this anthology features essays by Henry James, Kate Chopin, Willa Cather, Sinclair Lewis, Jack London, Raymond Chandler, Raymond Carver, Eudora Welty, and Kurt Vonnegut, Jr. 192pp. 5⅜ x 8½. 0-486-45128-3

HAMLET, William Shakespeare. The quintessential Shakespearean tragedy, whose highly charged confrontations and anguished soliloquies probe depths of human feeling rarely sounded in any art. Reprinted from an authoritative British edition complete with illuminating footnotes. 128pp. 5³⁄₁₆ x 8¼. 0-486-27278-8

THE HAUNTED HOUSE, Charles Dickens. A Yuletide gathering in an eerie country retreat provides the backdrop for Dickens and his friends — including Elizabeth Gaskell and Wilkie Collins — who take turns spinning supernatural yarns. 144pp. 5⅜ x 8½. 0-486-46309-5